A New Agenda for Family Support

Providing Services that Create Social Capital

Colm O'Doherty

BLACKHALL
Publishing

ISBN: 978-1-84218-138-6

A catalogue record for this book is available from the British Library.

This book was typeset by Paragon Prepress, Inc. for
Blackhall Publishing
33 Carysfort Avenue
Blackrock
Co. Dublin
Ireland.
e-mail: info@blackhallpublishing.com
www.blackhallpublishing.com

Printed in the UK by Athenaeum Press Ltd.

ACKNOWLEDGEMENTS

I am indebted to all those people who over the years have encouraged me to work and think about the positive value of social connections and personal relationships. Jerry Green, Rob Lorimer, Kevin Esmonde, Ger Phillips, Tom O'Connor and Bernie O'Carroll have all helped me to understand and appreciate the positive power of neighbourhoods and local solidarity.

I also wish to thank my colleagues in the ITT who provided such a supportive and stimulating environment in which to work on the book, particularly Tom Farrelly who offered considerable advice and Pat McGarty who has been helpful and encouraging throughout.

Finally, I would like to thank Elizabeth Brennan, whose considerable efforts in producing the final manuscript were invaluable.

To – Anna, Ellen, Luke and Molly for patience, encouragement and loving support; Donal and Dora for everything; Johnny Calnan (1969–2007) for seeing the best in life and sharing that with us all; Donal, Sean, Brian and Aine for their belief in me.

TABLE OF CONTENTS

INTRODUCTION

The intention of this book is to open up new avenues of practice for social work and social care professionals. It invites students and practitioners to take a wider view of their professional tasks and consider how they can incorporate a structured approach to the creation of well-being and social cohesion in their professional activities. Social care and social work are often characterised as 'helping' professions but their potential is not fully realised unless they take account of the holistic and interdependent nature of people's needs. What is called for in this book is practice that operates as a force for positive change at community and societal levels, while attending to the particular needs of individuals and families.

Simply put, family support is an active agent in the creation of healthy societies. Healthy societies encourage and facilitate all individuals and families to be as fully functioning as possible. Societies in which difference is valued and celebrated are likely to promote general well-being among the population. In societies where the emphasis is on the management or regulation of difference, social relations are determined by a culture of compliance rather than a culture of opportunity.

Essentially, family support is a renewable resource for social development and individual growth, which can be harnessed by citizens and professionals seeking springboards for positive human participation in everyday life. In this way family support has the potential to concern itself with welfare and well-being activities that are mutually beneficial to the individual and wider collective social organisations which have claims on them. To date in Ireland, the emphasis has been placed on the role of family support work in promoting welfare agendas. This is not to suggest that there is anything intrinsically 'unsound' about family support as an

1

instrument of welfare policy. However, this one-dimensional approach to family support practice in Ireland can be contrasted with the social development model, popular in France and Germany, which views family support, not as a means to a welfare end, but as an umbrella term describing long-term self-sustaining movements towards individual and social revitalisation. Within the welfare policy model, family support has been directed towards the provision of services for marginalised and disadvantaged individuals, families and communities. The focus has been on social exclusion rather than social inclusion. As a result of this policy approach, family support is perceived as a range of services for people with problems or difficulties rather than as an opportunity for citizens of mainstream society to participate in activities that expand their life chances and choices. A central theme of this book is that without the 'middle-class' buy-in necessary to establish and sustain it as a universal service, the beneficial potential of family support for civil society in Ireland has only been partially realised. To date, the declared aim of the Government's Family and Community Services Resource Centre programme is 'to help combat disadvantage by improving the functioning of the family unit' (Family Support Agency 2005: 4). Getting more resourceful citizens, as well as those who are disadvantaged, engaged in family support work would increase interactions between members of communities and 'create value, both by practices which increase the supply of "collective goods", such as facilities for overcoming conflicts and problems, for mutual support and shared enjoyment, and by contributions and exchanges which create a sense of loyalty, solidarity and belonging' (Jordan 2007: 108).

The broader perspective on family support activities which this book articulates can be conceptualised in two ways. Firstly, it can refer to any services, programmes and initiatives in the local area to which families have access. Secondly, it can refer to the social capital present in a community and the avenues created through systems of help, support, advice, guidance and general activities for growth in social capital to occur. In this new model social capital constitutes a wellspring for social energy which acts as a community resource. My chief aim in this book is to offer an introduction to family support and to guide the reader through key policy and practice issues confronting social care and social work professionals who wish to generate social capital and provide effective services. The reader, who may be a student, qualified practitioner or an academic, will be guided through different family support 'stories' with a view to developing an appreciation of how such stories are representative of the prevailing family support policies and practices in any given society. The interpretive medium of storytelling is preferred to the more functionalist approach of using case studies because, with it, the focus of attention is not just on what actually happened but is also on how people make sense of what happened. These stories will be critically examined in the light of the emergence of social capital as a crucial concept in our understanding of healthy groups and communities. Finally, the book will set out a new model of family support work for social care and social work practitioners. The new model will incorporate some international practice strategies currently being used in Australia, the US and the UK.

OVERVIEW OF THE BOOK

Chapter One, 'The Capital Story', introduces the reader to the concept of social capital and the growing international awareness of the benefits of social capital for well-being generally. It then sets out in more detail the ways in which social capital makes a difference to people's lives.

Chapter Two, 'The Changing Family Story', begins with a general definition of family support. It moves on to examine some of the challenges for family support practices in a changing social landscape.

Chapter Three, 'A Family Centre Story', provides the reader with an account of how a successful Irish community-based project has evolved and is providing services whilst generating social capital. Interviews recording the views and experiences of stakeholders in the centre are included in this chapter.

Chapter Four, 'Stories from Abroad', looks at family support practices in Australia and the UK and considers how different approaches can be operationalised on an international basis.

Chapter Five, 'Practice Stories', highlights the practice repertoires that may be useful for family-centred practitioners in the areas of social care and social work. Drawing from international examples of best practice, a new model for community-oriented family support practice, which recognises the contribution of social capital to well-being, is then presented.

Chapter Six, 'Verifying the Story', considers how the effectiveness of family support initiatives can be measured and how empirical evidence of the links between social capital and a range of health outcomes can be gathered.

The concluding chapter, 'Creating New Stories', revisits key themes that emerge throughout the book and maps out a future direction for family support policy and practice.

CHAPTER ONE

THE CAPITAL STORY

INTRODUCTION: THE PROMISE OF SOCIAL CAPITAL

Over the past two decades, the number of scientific studies detailing the importance of neighbourhoods in supporting parenting and promoting or inhibiting children's development in Canada, the US, the UK and Australia has grown (Brooks-Gunn *et al.* 1997; Kohen *et al.* 2002; Sampson *et al.* 2002; Edwards 2005 and 2006; Schoor 1997). However, the practice of welfare professionals, such as social workers and social care workers, has been slow to respond to research insights revealing the social and institutional mechanisms through which neighbourhoods affect children. New thinking that takes account of these studies tends towards the development of policies and practices based on the capacities, skills and assets of people and their neighbourhoods. International recognition of the importance of building and supporting communities has found expression in the concept of social capital. Accordingly, this chapter offers the reader a general introduction to the concept of social capital, and to its historical development, manifestations and effects. The central message in the pages to come is that social capital represents a major resource, which can play a key role in contributing to positive outcomes for children, their families and the communities in which they live.

Areas addressed in this chapter are:

- What is social capital?
- Principal social capital theories.
- Social capital and the well-being of the individual.

WHAT IS SOCIAL CAPITAL?

*Money was sometimes acquired mechanically, by simple accumula-
tion or, on the other hand, by some audacious coup crowned with
success. Essentially abstract, money was a concept in which neither
race, physical appearance, age, intelligence nor distinction played any
part, nothing in fact, but money.*

Michel Houellebecq, *Platform*

Accumulating money, the DNA of economic capital, is an activity which
requires no social investment or commitment. Money can be accumulated
through a banal stroke of luck or inheritance as well as by conventional
usage of intellect, talent, strength, courage or beauty. By contrast, social
capital is quintessentially a product of collective interaction. Generating
positive social capital is increasingly recognised by academics and professionals as a process that can create added social value from the raw material of human relationships. One of the unique features of social capital
is that it can be both a cause or generator of positive social outcomes and
an effect of positive social outcomes. Its contribution to the furtherance
of an improved social dimension in the day-to-day lives of citizens can
be measured and evaluated. According to the Commission on Social
Justice:

> Social capital consists of the institutions and relationships of a thriv-
> ing civil society – from networks of neighbours to extended families,
> community groups to religious organisations, local businesses to
> local public services, youth clubs to parent-teacher associations,
> playgroups to police on the beat. Where you live, who else lives
> there, and how they live their lives – co-operatively or selfishly, re-
> sponsibly or destructively – can be as important as personal resources
> in determining life chances. (1994: 307–8)

While social capital is conceptually and empirically complex and contestable – it has been described by authors from the various disciplines of education (Coleman 1988), political science (Putnam 1993) and sociology (Bourdieu 1986) – there is sufficient overlap between varying definitions to identify the main indicators of social capital as:

- social relationships and social support;
- formal and informal social networks;
- group memberships;
- community and civic engagement;
- norms and values;
- reciprocal activities (e.g. childcare arrangements);
- levels of trust in others.

In summary then:

> Communities have various types of resources. Alongside investment in roads, high technology and physical capital, investment in human skills and knowledge is important. The latter is frequently referred to as human capital in the sense that investments in human creativity and skill can generate economic wealth and human well-being. Social capital is an additional resource. It refers to the social ties, shared norms and relationships among people and communities. It acts like a social glue or lubricating agent in association with other forms of resources. (NESF 2003)

What is the story behind this concept? Why are academics, politicians and professionals across the globe interested in an intangible force which, its advocates claim, is capable of providing measurable returns for productive investment in social relations? The following section on the evolution of the theory of social capital from its first inception until recent times begins to answer these questions.

Beginning the Story – Durkheim and Bourdieu

Emile Durkheim (1858–1917) was a key figure in the creation of a coherent and scientific discipline in the nineteenth century – sociology. Durkheim honed in on the importance of solidarity as a factor in the development and maintenance of societies. He focused on the social ties that hold societies together and shape social order. Durkheim identified two forms of social solidarity and the social structures that accompanied them. The mechanical solidarity of pre-modern societies was a solidarity of resemblance; individuals were essentially alike and the basis of social order was a shared belief in law and religion. Thus, obedience to authority was inculcated and fostered by custom and practice that was grounded in similarities of status and routines.

Durkheim argued that, within modern industrial societies, consensus is derived from people's economic interdependence and their recognition of the merit of others' contributions. He coined the term 'organic solidarity' to describe how, as society changes, individuals become increasingly dependent on one another. As the division of labour increases, each person needs goods and services that others in different occupations can supply. Here, social order is not founded on similarity but rather on individuals pursuing different but complementary functions. When relationships of economic reciprocity and mutual dependency become the basis of an increasing interdependency, social consensus is not derived from shared beliefs. New economic relationships encourage interdependency but also promote individual thought and expression. In spite of individuals being unlike one another (in terms of their occupations, for instance), they can get on together because they are reliant on each other's services and skills in order for social life to work.

While Durkheim's analysis of the function of social connections in the creation of social solidarity preceded the debate on social capital, he identified a cohesive force that prevents societies from atomising.

Pierre Bourdieu was born in south-eastern France in 1930 and trained initially as a philosopher. His conscription into the French army and his experiences in the Algerian war were formative events in his life. He moved towards sociology via anthropology and, in the 1960s, he established himself as a leading sociologist in Paris. He identified tangible and intangible forms of economic, social and cultural assets which could be combined to create and reproduce inequality in society. He took issue with the conventional view that regarded economic assets as the paramount force in shaping social order:

> It is in fact impossible to account for the structure and functioning of the social world unless one reintroduces capital in all its forms and not solely in the one form recognised by economic theory. (1986: 422)

Bourdieu believed that, in addition to economic capital, due recognition must also be accorded to the importance of social and cultural capital in patterning social organisation and social practices.

Bourdieu's interest in the reproduction of inequality through the mechanism of culture found voice in his work on the various cultural advantages that can be turned into economic gains. By using the metaphor of cultural capital, he was able to explore and analyse the diverse foundations of social order. He drew attention to the different forms that cultural capital can take:

- The embodied state represents the culture that an individual has incorporated into their thinking and behaviour.
- The objectified state relates to culture that is accessed or found in 'things'. It is the culture that exists in and through material possessions such as books or painting or clothing.
- The institutionalised state is typically culture as represented in education or training certificates – certificates of 'cultural competence'.

Bourdieu pinpointed the manner in which this cultural capital (articulation, ideas, views, dress, possessions and educational achievements) interacts with economic and social capital in a way that enables some individuals to gain elevated positions in society. Social capital is an accumulation of assets which 'may accrue to an individual or a group by virtue of possessing a durable network of more-or-less institutionalised relationships of mutual acquaintance and recognition' (Bourdieu and Wacquant 1992: 119).

To accumulate social capital, individuals form ties and connections, often based on mutual obligations and reciprocity, which assist them in their daily lives. Membership of clubs, involvement in professional or political associations and occupational cliques provide gilt-edged opportunities for accumulation of 'high order' social capital. Involvement or membership of community or residents' associations and engagement in voluntary activities constitute mechanisms for the accumulation of 'lower order' social capital. While Bourdieu did not identify a hierarchy of social capital accumulation, he wrote about the phenomenon as it occurred in the upper echelons of French society. In this way, social capital functions to reproduce inequality and maintains a close but semi-independent relationship with economic and cultural capital.

It is important to acknowledge the weaknesses in Bourdieu's analysis of the role of social capital in the reproduction of inequality. He regarded social capital as a means whereby essentially law-abiding individuals could use their social connections to further their own interests. However, he did not extend his analysis to cover the possibility that criminals and other social 'outsiders' may just as easily engage in social capital accumulation which may be advantageous to them but disadvantageous to the maintenance of a specific social order. Bourdieu also viewed social capital accumulation as an individualistic enterprise and did not acknowledge the degree to which it can be regarded as a product of collective interaction.

The Story Continues – Coleman and Putnam

The American sociologist James Coleman was appointed director of a research programme established under the 1964 Civil Rights Act, which enquired into the origins of educational inequalities in America. His study confirmed that factors relating to the school itself, such as its material resources, made little difference to educational performance. The decisive influence on educational performance was the children's backgrounds:

> Inequalities imposed on children by their home, neighbourhood, and peer environment are carried along to become the inequalities with which they confront adult life at the end of school. (Coleman 1966: 325)

Coleman ascribed the basis of the differential patterns of achievement confirmed in his research studies to the impact of community norms upon parents and pupils, which reinforced teachers' expectations. This finding alerted him to the possibility that communities were a source of social capital which could act as a counterbalance to the economic and social disadvantages endured by families living in adverse circumstances. Coleman was, broadly speaking, attempting to bring together key ideas from economics and sociology in order to develop an interdisciplinary social science. Classical economic theory assumes that all behaviour stems from individuals pursuing their own interests. A strand of sociological enquiry known as rational choice theory is based on the same assumption.

Within this shared intellectual framework, all social interaction is characterised as a form of exchange. In their dealings with others, individuals can opt for competitive or co-operative forms of exchange. The overall function of all such interaction is assumed to be self-interest. By choosing to interact in ways which facilitate levels of co-operation, individuals pursuing their own self-interest can, on an involuntary basis, be contributing to the development of social capital, which in turn can be interpreted as a form of personal or human capital. Coleman attempted to show how the development of social capital is connected to the individual's accumulation of human capital. He regarded human and social capital as discrete but complementary elements of a functioning social order – a social order vested in structures promoting collective behaviours.

Robert Putnam's critical analysis of the factors influencing the effectiveness of regional government in Italy – *Making Democracy Work* (1993) – indicated that areas producing high levels of social capital supported more successful regional government than areas where the predominant forms of social organisation inhibited this process. Regional governments in the North of Italy were performing better than their counterparts in the South, as a result of the beneficial mutual interrelationship between government and civil society. A vibrant civil society (voluntary engagement between citizens in a community) and relatively high levels of trust between strangers in the North had evolved from the social patterns fostered by the activities of the early medieval guilds in the self-regulating city-states of the region. In the South, cultural practices did not promote such high levels of civic engagement. People inclined towards their kin for trust and support and were wary of participating in organisations with strangers. The governance structures in the South were more autocratic and less favourable for the development of associational life. Putnam took his analysis forward by relating the differences between regional administrations in the North and South of Italy to features of social organisation which were indicative of social capital formation:

> Social capital here refers to features of social organisation, such as trust norms and networks, that can improve the efficiency of society by facilitating co-ordinated actions. (Putnam 1993: 167)

His next major study focused on the parlous state of associational life in the US. With *Bowling Alone* (a title he gave to a book published in

2000 and a scholarly paper published in 1995), Putnam accounted for declining levels of social capital in America, gaining a measure of fame and capturing the attention of President Clinton. Putnam identified a downward trend in the membership rates of a whole range of local and national associations, from the parent-teacher associations to the Elks and labour unions. Putnam used secondary data sources such as the General Social Survey (conducted every two years since 1974), National Election studies (conducted every year since 1952), DDB Needham Life Style surveys (conducted annually since 1975) and the Social and Political Trends Survey (conducted by the Roper polling organisation), to tell the story of American social change. Much vaunted traditional pathways and frameworks for citizens to get to know each other and to collaborate socially in creating stocks of social capital are no longer lead players in the American story. Putnam entitled his story *Bowling Alone* in recognition of a shift in social patterns away from group involvement in recreational pursuits towards a more solitary, individualised perspective on populist perennial, quintessential American pastimes such as bowling. Factors influencing this withdrawal of increasing numbers of Americans from the social round include:

- The pace and pressures of day-to-day living reduce the time and energy available to people for participating in communal events, activities and pastimes. The focus for large sections of US citizens is on earning a living and little else.
- The spatial living arrangements which condemn residents of large metropolitan areas to a lifestyle of endless driving and fragmented social ties.
- Over-reliance of individuals on television and electronic mediums for entertainment and personal fulfilment.
- Intergenerational changes in social values impact on patterns of civic engagement. Those born in the 1920s belong to nearly twice as many associations as their descendants born in the 1960s. They are also twice as likely to vote and three times as likely to read a newspaper.

One of the major criticisms of Putnam's work is that it tells us the story of declining levels of social capital from the perspective of

Americans' withdrawal from formal associational life, but is less informative about informal social connections. However, commercial survey data obtained by the Putnam team in the late 1990s makes it clear that social interaction with friends, families and colleagues has not filled the gap created by withdrawal from clubs and formal associations. Americans are entertaining friends at home less frequently than they did in the 1970s. In the mid-1970s they entertained friends at home about fourteen to fifteen times a year but, by the late 1990s, they were entertaining only about eight times per year. A drop of 40–50 per cent in activities such as visiting friends, and going out to bars, night clubs, discos and taverns confirmed that this was a definite trend in patterns of social interaction. It doesn't appear as if Americans are becoming more family-oriented either. Families are not eating dinner together or going on holiday together as much as they used to. Work based sociability rates have also disimproved, with less reported satisfaction with time spent at work (44 per cent in 1955 and 16 per cent in 1999) as opposed to time away from work. While individual involvement in sports and fitness is on the increase, having nearly doubled between 1960 and 1998, participation in team sports has gone down by 10–20 per cent. Accelerating the trend towards a drying up of face-to-face informal social channels is the increasing use of telecommunications to initiate and maintain contact. However, the one-dimensional nature of telephone or e-mail contact restricts the development of trust (a basic component of social capital), and thereby militates against the creation of viable social capital.

It is in the key area of trust that these trends coalesce. Social trust is falling: in 1960, 55 per cent of Americans said that other people could generally be trusted, by 1998 this had fallen to 33 per cent. A corollary of this decline in informal trust has been an increase in specialised 'trust enforcers', with the numbers of police, guards and watchmen approximately doubling between 1960 and 1996. The numbers of lawyers and judges has more than doubled during this period.

This section has recounted the historical development of the influential concept of social capital. Despite their different starting points, all four major theorists recognise the importance of social ties in maintaining social order. A summary of the seminal perspectives of Durkheim, Bourdieu, Coleman and Putnam on social order and social capital is set out in Table 1.1.

TABLE 1.1: SOCIAL CAPITAL THEORISTS

	Social Order	Social Capital Formation	Social Cohesion
Durkheim	Mechanical and organic solidarity	People's social ties serve to knit a wider society together.	Continuation of society depends on co-operation, which in turn presumes a general consensus or agreement among its members over basic values.
Bourdieu	Social organisation and social practices are patterned by economic, social and cultural capital.	To accumulate social capital, individuals form ties and connections – often based on mutual obligations and reciprocity – which assist them in their daily lives.	Economic capital is at the root of all other types of capital. A social hierarchy is maintained and legitimated by the cultural capital of the upper and middle classes. Social capital is an asset of the privileged and a means of maintaining their superiority.
Coleman	Society is an aggregation of social systems of individual behaviour.	Actors do not set out to create social capital – it arises as an unintended consequence of their pursuit of self-interest.	Social capital, as a public good, provides a set of norms and sanctions (standards and penalties) that allow individuals to co-operate for mutual advantage.
Putnam	Civic engagement generates political stability and economic prosperity.	Participation in civil society (voluntary organisations, clubs, associations).	Social cohesion is produced by three primary features of social life – networks, norms, trust – that enable participants to act together to pursue shared objectives more effectively.

SOCIAL CAPITAL AND WELL-BEING

Having established that America's social capital is in decline, Putnam demonstrated the existence of a relationship between social capital and indicators of well-being such as education, economic prosperity, health, happiness and democratic engagement. In order to do this, he combined fourteen separate measures or indicators of social capital into a single Social Capital Index, which he then used to illustrate the spread of social capital across the fifty American states. Measures or indicators such as levels of social trust and engagement in civic affairs were aggregated to produce the Social Capital Index. This exercise showed that some states had higher social capital levels than others. Across a range of indicators of well-being, states such as Mississippi, Alabama and Louisiana do not rate as highly as states such as Minnesota, Iowa and the New England state of Vermont.

Durkheim's ground-breaking work into the social nature of suicide (1952) established a relationship between social cohesion and health. In the late nineteenth century, Durkheim demonstrated that suicide rates were related to levels of social integration. Higher rates were found in populations with low levels of social integration and lower rates in more closely bound communities. Subsequent studies have signposted a broadly positive relationship between social capital and health. At the micro or individual level, cross-sectional studies have identified a strong association between the extent and value of people's social networks and their health.

Those people who are less socially isolated and more involved in social and civic activities are likely to have better health (F.E. Baum *et al.* 2000; Veenstra 2000). Mental health, happiness and physical health, according to a range of studies (see Chapter Three in Halpern (2005) for details), can be enhanced, supported and protected when individuals can access rewarding, intimate personal relationships through social networks. At the meso or community level, evidence of a more general association between health levels and social ties has existed since the late 1970s, which indicates that people with strong social networks had mortality rates of half or a third of those with weak social ties (Whitehead and Diderichsen 2001). The Irish Government's mental health strategy, outlined in the report *A Vision for Change* (2006), accepts that factors associated with inadequate social capital are found to have an independent negative effect on mental health. Such factors include:

- lack of neighbourhood trust;
- a high level of problems in the local area;
- a poor level of local services;
- infrequent contact with friends;
- lack of social support.

It can be argued that the health benefits often stem from the quality of an individual's personal support system (intimate relationships and friendships) rather than membership of a strong cohesive community. Halpern is sceptical that a person's health and well-being can be enhanced as much through membership of a social grouping as through personal relationships:

> It is one thing to say that individuals who have supportive friendships at work or in the neighbourhood tend to be happier and healthier. But it is another to say that some firms or neighbourhoods create such a positive atmosphere that the average level of well-being is increased more than could have been expected from each individual's circumstances. (2005: 87)

However, individuals' health choices are influenced by the lifestyle of people they trust and the effectiveness of social capital depends heavily on community approaches and perspectives on health maintenance and promotion. Where communities embrace lifestyles that promote health and discourage negative or risky behaviours, such as cigarette smoking, alcohol consumption and poor diet, then membership of this community is likely to benefit your health. It is also important to state that social capital alone cannot produce positive health outcomes. Socio-economic situation and income are critically important predictors of health levels, as has been suggested by English health survey research (Cooper *et al.* 1999). Social capital is an important variable in the health and well-being equation and well-networked communities often exhibit greater prosperity than restricted or small-scale networks (Field 2003: 59). This may indicate that some networks are better than others at promoting healthy behaviour. Membership of these well-networked communities may not be available to all comers. Barriers to membership may be linked to income and ethnic factors.

At the macro or national level, happiness and life satisfaction data are strongly supportive of the effects of social capital on well-being. Putnam's research produced a correlation at state level between a range of health indicators and his Social Capital Index. He advanced four possible reasons for the link between social capital and health (2000: 327):

1. Social networks can help to secure tangible material assistance and thereby reduce stress.
2. Social networks can reinforce healthy norms.
3. Social networks provide a platform for active engagement in lobbying campaigns for medical services.
4. Social networks provide positive opportunities for social interaction which may stimulate the body's immune system.

Halpern (2005) suggests that social capital at the nation state level is manifested through the quality of day-to-day relationships between citizens. Those living in 'high-trust' (an outcome of social capital which is desirable for economic success – see Fukuyama 1995) states and regions may generally be 'nicer' to one another. Social capital may be instrumental in promoting such a culture of civility and respect. The pattern of exchange between friends and strangers in this type of social order is generally less stressful – friends and strangers may be more pleasant and civil to one another, making life easier and less conflictual. In this way, a virtuous social environment is created where people are more inclined to support each other and enter into positive reciprocal relationships with strangers (for example, they might stop and give directions to strangers). States with high social trust may also produce more beneficial health and well-being because they have better public services:

Government investments in hospitals, welfare provision and public utilities are all thought to have a substantial impact on population health, a view supported by Lynch *et al.* (Muntaner *et al.* 2002). But once again the case has been made that there is a strong reciprocal relationship between state-level social capital and government performance and its ability to develop and implement policy, and between economic inequality and the strength of the welfare state.

It is certainly the case that across US metropolitan areas, areas with high social capital report better access to health care (Hendryx *et al.*, 2002). Across policy areas, the argument has been made that higher social capital leads to higher support and more effective lobbying for public services. (Halpern 2005: 107–108)

According to Richard Wilkinson, the story of social capital and health and well-being at a national or macro level is essentially a commentary on levels of inequality existing within different societies. Wilkinson (1996) and Kawachi *et al.* (1997) identify a broad association between health and social cohesion. Research into inequality across the US uncovered a close relationship between income inequality, social mistrust and mortality (Kawachi *et al.* 1997). In other words, inequality generates social mistrust and social mistrust in turn generates poorer population health. Wilkinson's study of the effects of relative inequality on health and well-being in wealthy nations turned up some evidence to support the proposition that social inequality tends to reduce social stability and undermine social networks. While absolute wealth or poverty determines the ability to buy goods, relative inequality may consign an individual to a low status position in society with a higher risk of poverty, social exclusion and stress. Within nations organised around a hierarchical system of inequality, power and coercion provide access to resources regardless of the needs of others. Nations which are more equal are less reliant on power and coercion as a means of maintaining social order and are characterised by more co-operative social relations. Wilkinson argues that, in more equal nations, people's needs are more readily recognised and mediated through obligations of sharing and reciprocity:

> Societies which are both egalitarian and healthy are also markedly more socially cohesive than others. Above all, the public sphere in these societies seemed to be incorporated in social life rather than being abandoned to the negative market relations between self-interested households. With reduced income inequality, people are connected in public life through a variety of social organisations, purposes and activities. (Wilkinson 1996: 213)

Social Capital and Crime

Crime and Deviancy

Criminal behaviour transgresses a set of specific rules codified within the legal system. Deviance may be defined as the infraction of any agreed-upon social rule or expectation and, as such, it is a broader concept than crime. For many sociologists, the central fact about deviance is that it is created by society. Crime is a major realm of societal concern, whereas deviance in day-to-day behaviour may be tolerated and even encouraged in artistic and cultural lifestyles. As Marsh *et al.* put it:

> Crime may be defined as an act that breaks the criminal law; it can be followed by criminal proceedings and formal punishment. ... Deviance is a less precise concept than crime; deviance means any behaviour that differs from the normal. Thus, deviant behaviour could be uncommonly good or brave behaviour as well as unacceptable behaviour, such as theft or vandalism. (2000: 656)

Sociological theories relating to crime and deviance may be classified under the following headings.

Functionalist Theories

Common to all functionalist-based theory is the significance of shared norms (norms represent the 'dos' and 'don'ts' of social life) and values which form the basis of social order. Durkheim argued that deviance, and an average rate of crime in particular, was a normal phenomenon in a society. His argument may seem strange, given that crime involves breaking laws, but it rests on the assumption that the rate of crime in any society is an indication of the balance struck between individualism (pursuit of self-interest) and social regulation (imposition of collective rules and values on individuals). Where the balance is evenly struck between these two positions, then an average rate of crime may be expected. In most societies the balance is out of kilter, producing either low rates of crime (when there is too much regulation of the individual by society) or high rates of crime (when individualism becomes uncontrolled). Robert Merton (1957) suggested that criminal behaviour results from a contradiction between the aspirations or goals into which society has socialised people (in Western society material success is a generally held goal) and the ways that are provided for the realization of these aspirations (the means).

Social Dislocation Theories

Social dislocation occurs as a result of changes in a society that undermine and weaken formal and informal forms of traditional authority such as family, Church and local community. Modernisation, like any other form of social change, weakens the capacity of traditional forms of authority to exert control over behaviour. As societies modernise, old jobs disappear and people have to become more mobile in order to find work. Increased crime is an inevitable result of this erosion of the shared values that previously maintained order.

Social Capital and Crime

> The picture that emerges from both the official statistics and the small amount of available research could be summarised as follows: the bulk of the crime committed in contemporary Ireland is still relatively small-scale property crime and the property attacked is mainly that of younger middle-class people, while those who attack it are very young males from working-class backgrounds who have little chance of integrating into stable and rewarding jobs and lives. We might be tempted to conclude that, in a society where the state has generally intervened to redistribute resources from those with little to those with quite a lot, crime offers an alternative resource redistribution from those with quite a lot to those with very little. (Tovey and Share 2003: 306)

While it is always difficult to fully explain the complex relationship between the social circumstances of a young person and their involvement or non-involvement in criminal activity, substantial evidence has been uncovered to highlight the importance of social networks in the equation. Young people who are connected to mainstream social networks are subject to informal social control and the consequent internalising of certain norms that may forestall offending. During adolescence, a young person will be 'in transit' between the restraining influences of her or his family and the wider social ties that are linked to employment, further education and intimate adult relationships. A great deal of research conducted into offending behaviour has sought to explain why some young people experiment with crime during adolescence but desist dramatically as they enter adulthood, while others embark on long-term criminal careers. Sampson and Laub, in their re-analysis of the life-history data of a sample of 500 convicted teenage offenders and 500 non-delinquents from the 1940s and 1950s, found that: 'social ties ... create interdependent systems of obligation and restraint that impose significant costs for translating criminal propensities into action'(1993: 141).

In this analysis, social ties are seen as an incentive for self-regulation in order to achieve a measure of self-fulfilment in the adult world and mainstream society. However, the mediating influence of positive social ties on leading young persons away from crime is strengthened or weakened by antecedent factors located in their families and neighbourhoods. For instance, there is a strong association between material inequality and criminal behaviour. Inequality, rather than poverty, appears to be a major source of such behaviour (Halpern 2005). Disrupted and unstable family backgrounds and the individual's overall social context operate in tandem with each other to engineer a loose reinforcement 'between the individual's social context and their evolving character and lifestyle. But this is not a fully deterministic relationship. A chance encounter or positive relationship can change the person's life course dramatically' (Halpern 2005: 116).

A positive relationship or set of relationships can offset the effects of adverse social circumstances and prevent offending. Equally, connection to a deviant or criminal social network can result in a young person acquiring 'criminal capital' (Hagan and McCarthy 1997). I will return to social capital's 'dark side' later in this chapter.

At the meso or community level, as Halpern (2005: 123) has succinctly put it, 'crime can be expected to be higher where there are large numbers of potential offenders in close proximity to large numbers of victims' (2005: 123). In their analysis of the British Crime Survey, Aitchison and Hodgkinson (2003) identified two neighbourhood types – 'striving' and 'rising' areas – which are more susceptible to crime. Typically, 'striving' areas are populated by welfare recipients such as lone parents, the elderly, asylum seekers and refugees, the unemployed and immigrants. These populations may be residing in local authority housing estates or privately rented accommodation. 'Rising' areas are largely inhabited by well-off professionals and singles. The common denominator between theses two areas is low social capital. With regard to these factors, a key question to be addressed is whether or not there is a 'neighbourhood effect' at work here. Can the heightened levels of crime in these areas be put down to individual-level variables, such as the concentration of offenders in their populations, or is there evidence that something more is happening at the neighbourhood level that can be attributed to the sum of the parts – an ecological-level effect. Ecological theories focus on the behaviour of individuals and families as a function of their adaptation to the broader social context. As Putman argues:

> The presence of lots of stable families in a neighbourhood is as-sociated with lower levels of youthful lawbreaking, not because the adults serve as role models or supervisors, but because the adults rear well-adjusted and well-behaved kids. Thus 'good families' have a ripple effect by increasing the pool of 'good peers' that that other families' kids can befriend. If we think of youthful troublemaking as a communicable disease – a sort of behavioural chicken pox that spreads through high schools and friendship groups – then stable families provide the vaccines that reduce the number of contagious kids capable of infecting others. (2000: 314)

Extensive studies on crime and anti-social behaviour have produced ecological theories emphasising the role of 'positive externalities' (family social capital spilling out of the home and into the streets) in the creation of neighbourhood moral cohesion (see Putnam 2000: 307–318). However, the introduction of the Anti-Social Behaviour Act 2003 in the UK and the growing political support for similar legislation to be introduced in Ireland suggests that, at the national or macro level, dealing with the strain on the social fabric is being processed at the individual rather than the neighbourhood level. Constituting as they do a reductionist populist approach to the vexed problem of 'bad behaviour' and unsafe neighbour-hoods, such approaches are politically appealing because they appear to offer a degree of regulation and moral certainty to socially disorganised communities within a short timeframe. It can be argued that anti-social behaviour orders, curfews and parenting orders will lead to negative so-cial capital formation, maintenance and sustainability. The pull of what Putnam (2000) has termed 'the dark side of social capital' for young people and adults is strengthened by the labelling of them as deviants. According to Becker:

> Social groups create deviance by making the rules whose infraction constitutes deviance, and by applying those rules to particular people and labelling them as outsiders. From this point of view deviance is not a quality of the act the person commits, but rather a consequence of the application by others of rules and sanctions to an 'offender'. The deviant is one to whom the label has successfully been applied; deviant behaviour is behaviour that people so label. (1963)

In turning towards sanctions-led approaches to the perceived coarsening of public life, a society may be shifting its centre of gravity from tolerance towards intolerance. Societies grounded in tolerance offer more fertile conditions for the cultivation of social capital. Table 1.2 illustrates the relationship between tolerance and social capital.

TABLE 1.2: TOLERANCE AND SOCIAL CAPITAL

	Low Social Capital	High Social Capital
High Tolerance	1. Individualistic: 'You do your thing and I'll do mine.'	3. Civic community: (Salem without 'witches').
Low Tolerance	2. Anarchic: War of all against all.	4. Sectarian community: ('in-group' versus 'out-group'; Salem with 'witches').

Source: Putnam, R.D. (2000), *Bowling Alone – The Collapse and Revival of American Community,* New York: Simon and Schuster.

Putnam suggests that an individual's greater capacity for social interaction can be explained by pre-existing higher tolerance levels:

> Social joiners and civic activists are as a rule more tolerant of dissent and unconventional behaviour than social isolates are, a pattern first discovered by social scientists during the repressive McCarthy period of the 1950s and repeatedly confirmed since then. (2000: 355)

At the crux of this debate is the re-branding of some unconventional behaviour as anti-social behaviour. With little or no across-the-board agreement on what constitutes anti-social behaviour – defined by the Crime and Disorder Act 1998 as acts likely to cause 'harassment, alarm, or distress to one or more persons not in the same household' – the scene is set for the random demonising of sections of society by antagonistic others. The following newspaper articles give an example of 'demonising' processes.

Banning the 'Hoodie'

Fashion Item or Symbol of Fear?

The zip on 14-year-old Sophie's white hooded top is pulled fashionably low, showing of her gold chains as she talks. She and her mates, hanging around McDonalds on the Crayford roundabout in Kent, may look a little intimidating – one is being sick; cigarettes and cans of lager are freely shared – but they are adamant there is nothing to fear. Besides, she argues, the ban on wearing 'hoodies' imposed last week by the local Bluewater shopping centre, triggering a national debate over behaviour is illogical. 'I wouldn't mind, but they sell all these tops in Bluewater. Why don't they stop selling them before they ban them?'
The Observer, 15 May 2005

Ban 'Hoodies' from Shopping Centres

Former Fine Gael leader Michael Noonan has suggested shopping centre managers should ban people wearing hooded tops on their premises to reduce shoplifting. Mr. Noonan, Fine Gael TD for Limerick East, said most shoplifters wore hooded tops because camera security systems were largely ineffective in identifying people wearing hoods. 'Most shoplifting according to gardaí, in shopping centres and shopping malls is now being undertaken by people wearing hoods, usually younger people, both male and female. Security systems which are dependent on cameras are largely ineffective in identifying a person who shoplifts wearing a hood.' A Limerick shopping centre has already introduced a ban on hooded tops, Mr Noonan said, and with great success.
Irish Times, 10 November 2005

SOCIAL CAPITAL'S CAPACITY FOR NEGATIVE OUTCOMES

Negative social outcomes, which legal instruments such as anti-social behaviour orders are intended to curb, may be influenced by a type of social capital which supports and produces inward-looking social networks. Referred to as 'bonding' social capital, it reinforces solidarity and ties between homogenous groups. As such, it can be utilised at one end of the spectrum by nefarious organisations such as the Mafia or the Klu Klux Klan and at the other end by golf clubs that foster exclusivity. In between these two extremes it can underpin golden circles of exploitative individuals or sustain the strong ties between families, ethnic groups and immigrant communities. 'Bridging' social capital, on the other hand, enables participation and involvement in outward-looking networks, such as the civil rights movement in the US, to take place. 'Linking' social capital 'consists of relationships up and down the social and economic scale ... the importance of linking social capital is that it allows people to leverage resources, ideas and information from contacts outside their own social milieu. This idea has particular practical importance for community development policies and other anti-poverty strategies' (Field 2003: 66). In summary then, bonding social capital is good for 'getting by', bridging social capital is good for 'getting ahead' and linking social capital leverages empowering resources. In day-to-day life social networks may be sources of both bridging and bonding social capital. Putman argues:

> Many groups simultaneously bond along some social dimensions and bridge across others. The black church, for example, brings together people of the same race and religion across class lines. The Knights of Columbanus was created to bridge cleavages among different ethnic communities while bonding along religious and gender lines. Internet chat groups may bridge across geography, gender, age and religion while being tightly homogenous in education and ideology. In short, bonding and bridging are not 'either/or' categories into which social networks can be neatly divided but 'more or less' dimensions along which we can compare different forms of social capital. (2000: 23)

Savage (2005) contends that, contrary to Putnam's thesis, research indicates that associational social capital tends to be of the bonding rather than the bridging variety. His study of people's local identity, leisure practices, lifestyles and the kind of social ties produced by these understandings and interactions revealed that membership of associations was a means to evoke distinctions between insiders and outsiders. Associations, in the context of four contrasting areas near Manchester, were regarded as breeding grounds of social divisions based on elitism and snobbery. Instead of contributing to social cohesion by helping to create bridging social capital options, these associations were encouraging members to bond in an exclusive manner.

SOCIAL CAPITAL AND ECONOMIC PERFORMANCE

On the micro or individual level, being connected to a vibrant network is a good starting point for finding a new position or gaining a promotion. University graduates and internet entrepreneurs are examples of individuals whose networking abilities can enhance their career prospects. The dictum 'it's not what you know but who you know that matters when it comes to getting ahead' is a particularly good summary of the effect of social capital at the individual or micro level. Individuals who can capitalise on educational opportunities will build up their stock of human capital and thereby enhance their labour market value. Educational starting

TABLE 1.3: A MATRIX OF HUMAN AND SOCIAL CAPITAL COMPONENTS

Type of Capital	Human	Social (informal)	Social (formal)
Type of Trust	Trust in ourselves	Trust in each other	Trust in organisations
Components	Self-esteem	Level of trust	Number of organisations
	Self-respect	Norms	
	Self-confidence	Reciprocity	Services provided
	Attitudes	Networks and connections	Effectiveness
	Skills and knowledge		Community involvement
	Behaviour		Networks and partnerships

Source: Baron, S. *et al.* (2000), *Social Capital: Critical Perspectives*, Oxford: Oxford University Press.

points are critically important when it comes to amassing human capital, the raw material for the formation of social capital. Table 1.3 illustrates the component parts of human and social capital.

As Putnam has expressed it – 'People who grow up in well-to-do families with economically valuable social ties are more likely to succeed in the economic marketplace, not merely because they tend to be richer and better educated, but because they can and will ply their connections' (2000: 319). However Granovetter's study of how people find work, *Getting a Job* (1974), showed that job information was acquired accidentally, whenever contacts volunteered it. The most important sources of information on job opportunities were work or work-related contacts. Rarely were they part of the person's close network, i.e. family and friends. They tended to be people who were in different occupations to the respondent. On this evidence, Granovetter argues for the 'the strength of weak ties'. Overlapping contacts are a feature of close networks brought about by strong ties. Members of such networks have a tendency to be in possession of the same knowledge about job opportunities. They are all likely to get the same information and they are less likely to be sources of new information from more distant parts of their network or from separate networks. So the relatively weak ties of less frequent contacts and of people in different work situations are more likely to yield new and different information on job opportunities. As a result, 'acquaintances are more likely to pass job information than close friends' (Granovetter, 1974: 54).

At the meso or neighbourhood level, Halpern (2005) draws attention to the negative cycle which can be set up in disadvantaged neighbourhoods. Young people in these neighbourhoods are disconnected from advantaged individuals in mainstream employment and are largely unaware of job opportunities only a few miles away. Even when they are aware of the jobs, they do not apply because they lack 'trust in themselves' and 'trust in others' (see Table 1.3). Under these circumstances, social networks and norms, and particularly the dearth of connections to successful labour market participants, becomes self-reinforcing at the neighbourhood level. In contrast, when members of a disadvantaged community access wider opportunities for work and economic progression – such as through temporary economic migrations – they can act as a powerful bridge to new sources of affluence.

On the macro level, Fukuyama (1995) argues that successful economies are marked by the existence of high levels of social trust and its offshoot – social capital – amongst citizens. Putnam supports Fukuyama's contention that, when trust is absent or limited, significant costs are incurred and potential benefits are lost:

> When we can't trust our employees or other market players, we end up squandering our wealth on surveillance equipment, compliance structures, insurance, legal services, and enforcement of government regulations. Conversely, studies of the biotech industry by organization theorists like Walter Powell and Jane Fountain have shown that social networks that embody a norm of reciprocity – that is, social capital – are 'key enablers' of innovation, mutual learning and productivity growth, as important as physical and human capital, particularly in rapidly evolving fields. (2000: 325)

SOCIAL CAPITAL AND EDUCATION

While level of educational attainment is the strongest predictor of social capital in terms of civic engagement (Hall 1999; Putnam 2000), social capital helps to foster educational attainment. Furthermore, the evidence suggests that social capital at micro (individual or family), meso (neighbourhood or community), and macro (societal) levels has an important impact on educational outcomes:

- At the micro level, the quality of a child's interactions with his or her parents and the parents' social capital can positively affect the child's educational outcome.
- At the meso level, the type of school and the type of social capital it generates (based on strong parent-school and parent-parent relationships), coupled with the social capital of the community, can positively or negatively impact on a child's educational attainment. Where a neighbourhood is populated by families with low social capital, the overall low social capital of the community adds to the child's educational disadvantage, creating what Halpern terms 'a double jeopardy effect' (2005: 168).

- 'The macro-level reveals evidence of a startlingly strong relationship between social capital and educational attainment. Across US states, UK local authorities and nations, measures of social capital are strongly correlated with educational attainment, and these relationships are not explained by statistical controls for other variables such as wealth.' (Halpern 2005: 168)

CONCLUSION

The complex story behind the expanding usage of social capital as a term has been outlined in this chapter. Durkheim's examination of social order and its component parts established the importance of solidarity as a pre-requisite for a functioning society. Bourdieu, Coleman and Putnam, in their respective fields, sought to capture, through the concept of social capital, the everyday fabric of connection and tacit co-operation which can sustain social cohesion and promote solidarity. As a result of their work, it is possible to deconstruct the field of social capital into three major cross-cutting dimensions:

1. Components – networks, norms and sanctions.
2. Levels or domains of analysis – individuals, group, community, nation etc.
3. Character or function – bonding, bridging, linking.

Table 1.4 maps out the different levels, functions and dimensions of social capital.
The growing awareness of the benefits of social capital in promoting health and well-being, reducing levels of crime and improving economic performance have been set out.

This chapter has also assembled evidence for social capital being based on the concept of social connections as community resources, a proposition that informs the arguments that follow in this book. The next chapter considers how interventions seeking to improve the well-being of parents and children can support and draw upon the component parts of social capital – networks, social ties and mutual obligations – in ways that produce personal, economic and social gains.

TABLE 1.4: A CONCEPTUAL MAP OF SOCIAL CAPITAL, WITH EXAMPLES

Bonding	Bridging	Linking	
Macro level			
Honours and law	Diplomacy, war	International law	*Sanctions*
Patriotism and trust	Treaties	Human rights, aid	*Norms*
Nation or race	Trading links etc.	UN etc.	*Networks*
Meso level			
Exclusion	Group conflict	Enforcement	*Sanctions*
Community customs	Out-group understanding	Mutual respect	*Norms*
Neighbourhood or workplace	Links between communities	Links between strata	*Networks*
Micro level			
Withdrawal of affection	Shame and reputation	Shaming and formal sanction	*Sanctions*
Love and care	Reciprocity etc.	Generosity	*Norms*
Parents, siblings etc.	Acquaintances, friends etc.	Links to powerful	*Networks*

Source: Adapted from Halpern, D. (2005), *Social Capital,* Cambridge: Polity Press.

CHAPTER TWO

THE CHANGING FAMILY STORY

In the first instance, this chapter aims to offer a broad introduction to tangible and intangible resources and social support that make parenting an easier and more rewarding activity. Secondly, it also aims to relate these support processes to the ongoing changes affecting children and their parents. Areas addressed in this chapter include:

- Defining family support.
- New families.
- The best interests of the child.
- Families as social welfare organisations.
- A systems theory understanding of families.
- An ecological understanding of families as social welfare organisations.
- Supporting families as social welfare institutions.

DEFINING FAMILY SUPPORT – AN UMBRELLA TERM

Family support is best understood as an umbrella term describing a general movement rather than a unified approach to community development that promotes child and family welfare. The British Audit Commission (1994), Robbie Gilligan (1995), and Jack and Gill (2003) provide us with handy definitions that tell us part of the story. According to the British Audit Commission (1994):

Family support is any activity or facility provided either by statutory agencies or by community groups or individuals, aimed at providing advice and support to parents to help them in bringing up their children.

Robbie Gilligan (1995) has put forward a threefold functional categorisation of what is termed 'formal family support'. His typology acknowledges that family support may firstly be available through informal channels of kin, neighbours and friends. Formal services may be operated and instituted by social care or social work practitioners, public health nurses, youth workers and community workers. Gilligan's first category of formal family support – developmental family support – is manifested as a range of measures (e.g. personal development groups, recreational projects, youth programmes, parent education or adult education) relevant to social inclusion objectives. His second category is compensatory family support measures (e.g. pre-schools with intensive programmes for children from disadvantaged backgrounds and specialist youth programmes), which are geared towards counteracting the effects of social exclusion. In the third category, interventions are intended to offer protective family support to adults and children who are identified as being at risk (e.g. respite care for children in families with addiction problems, refuges and support groups for victims of domestic violence and programmes for parents lacking basic parenting skills).

SCOPE OF FAMILY SUPPORT

Types of Social Support

Basic Practical Support: help with childcare arrangements, e.g. a neighbour who is not working might provide after-school care for a working neighbour.

Emotional Support: listening and communicating. Listening is a skill which requires cultural awareness and understanding.

Esteem Support: If I esteem someone positively I will do so for their being kind or fair, brave or bold, a good parent, a conscientious colleague; or, in a more egocentrically focused way, for their being kind or fair, a good

parent or a conscientious colleague in their dea'
and Petit 2004).

Family Support Building Blocks

Values: social trust, reciprocity and inclusion.

Networks:
- Bonding – based on enduring, multi-faceted relationship.
  between similar people with strong mutual commitments,
  such as among friends, family and other close-knit groups.
- Bridging – formed from the connections between people who
  have less in common but may have an overlapping interest,
  for example between neighbours, colleagues or between different groups within a community.
- Linking – 'derived from the links between people or organisations beyond peer boundaries, cutting across status and
  similarity and enabling people to exert influence outside their
  normal circles' (Gilchrist 2004: 6).

Family Support Definitions:

- 'Integrated programmes combining statutory, voluntary,
  community and private sectors;
- positive reinforcement for informal social networks;
- targeting of the hard-to-reach vulnerable, or at-risk;
- wide range of activities and types of services;
- early intervention across a range of levels and needs;
- style of work based on operational and practice principles;
- promotion and protection of health, well-being and rights.'
  (Dolan *et al.* 2006: 16)

Family Support Practice Principles:

- Working in partnership is an integral part of family support.
  Partnership includes children, families, professionals and
  communities.
- Family support interventions are needs-led and strive for the
  minimum intervention required.

- Family support requires a clear focus on the wishes, feelings, safety and well-being of children.
- Family support services reflect a strengths-based perspective which is mindful of resilience as a characteristic of many children's and families' lives.
- Family support promotes the view that effective interventions are those that strengthen informal support networks.
- Family support is accessible and flexible in respect of location, timing, setting and changing needs and can incorporate both child protection and out-of-home care.
- Involvement of service users and providers in the planning, delivery and evaluation of family support services is promoted on an ongoing basis.
- Services aim to promote social inclusion, addressing issues around ethnicity, disability and rural or urban communities. (Dolan *et al.* 2006)

FAMILY SUPPORT RESOURCES

Jack and Gill (2003) organise the main resources which come under the heading of family support into three categories, as follows:

1. Formal Family Support Services:

- Personal social services delivered by social workers, family support workers and community childcare workers. In Ireland these services are currently provided by health board personnel.
- Structured individual or group support from a family or resource or health centre base. Springboard initiatives are an example of this kind of provision in the Irish context. In the UK, Surestart and Newpin projects can be identified as relevant services here.
- Structured support from health service personnel – public health nurses (Ireland) and health visitors (UK) provide these services.

2. Semi-Formal Family Support Services:

- Groups geared towards particular parenting activities such as nutrition.
- Men or women's personal development, issue-based or activity-focused groups, e.g. men overcoming violence groups.
- Domiciliary befriending volunteer projects, e.g. Homestart.
- Parent capacity building programmes put on by health boards, family centres and community groups, e.g. Parenting Plus.
- Groups for parents of children with specific childcare needs, e.g. disability groups.
- Luncheon clubs for older people, e.g. Cumann Iosaef in Tralee, Co. Kerry.

3. Informal Family Support Services:

- Cultural activities (music classes, drama groups, literary groups, sport and outdoor pursuits) which are accessible to parents and children in their neighbourhood or locality, e.g. Kerry Dioscesan Youth Services.
- Playgrounds and play facilities sited in convenient community sites, e.g. parent and toddler groups, toy libraries.
- Drop-in centres run on gender or ethnic lines (e.g. Trasnet Tralee, Tralee Women's Resource Centre), facilitated by the Health Service Executive, family centres and voluntary organisations.

These definitions are helpful in sketching out the role of different players in the family support story but they tell us little about family support as an arena for social change. Family support can be understood as a force for transformative social change as it reconnects individuals to communities and thereby enables both the individual and wider collectivity to generate positive social capital. In order to explain how this change can come about, we need to begin by examining social storylines that influence our day-to-day lives.

New Families

The typical West of Ireland family consists of father, mother, twelve children and resident Dutch anthropologist.

Flann O'Brien – attributed

Ulrich Beck, a prominent sociologist and chronicler of the changing nature of family, work, personal and cultural identity, has written that 'individual self-fulfilment and achievement is the most powerful current in modern society' (Beck 2000: 165). Members of the new evolving family no longer stick to traditional social storylines but ad-lib their way through a network society. In a network society friendship ties are as important as kin ties and individuals can opt for an 'open' family membership which does not cut across their involvement in wider networks. As a result, an individual's participation in family life is not fixed by traditional norms or social rules. Personal growth and autonomy agendas must now be accommodated within a family structure. One-size-fits-all family structures no longer endure. The concept of family now embraces two-parent, one-parent, married and unmarried arrangements. Adults parent together or separately and may be parenting their own children or children from a partner's previous relationship. Family life has become a means to a variety of ends rather than being an end in itself.

In the Irish context, a government policy document, *Strengthening Families for Life* (1998), refers to the following 'essential truths' about families:

- The family unit is a fundamental unit providing stability and well-being in our society.
- The unique and essential family function is that of caring for and nurturing all its members.
- Continuity and stability are major requirements in family relationships.
- An equality of well-being is recognised between individual family members.
- Family membership confers rights, duties and responsibilities.
- A diversity of family forms and relationships should be recognised.

These 'essential truths' provide us with understandings of family which are in harmony with the 'communitarian family' model as set out by the American academic Amitai Etzioni. In Etzioni's model, families are communities within communities. Families are the building blocks of community. As Frazer, commenting on the communitarian model, has put it, 'Familes are, ideally at least, communities, and conversely the idea of community is analysed as "family writ large"' (1999).

However Etzioni has a traditional view on the type of family form best suited to building healthy communities and societies. He conceptualises the family as a two-parent operation with both partners deeply and actively involved in the upbringing of children and all family members actively participating in community life.

The United Nations definition of the family (accepted by the Irish Government in the International Year of the Family, 1994) is broader and more reflective of the culturally diverse nature of contemporary Irish society:

> The family is any combination of two or more persons who are bound together by ties of mutual consent, birth and/or adoption or placement and who, together, assume responsibility for, *inter alia*, the care and maintenance of group members, the addition of new members through procreation or adoption, the socialisation of children, and the social control of members. (Cited in Commission on the Family 1998: 530)

The gathering momentum for change in the legal definition of family in Ireland has, in recent times, been highlighted by a legal challenge initiated by two women who married in Canada in 2003. They began legal proceedings in Ireland in an attempt to gain recognition for same-sex marriages and to thereby extend the rights of same-sex couples in matters relating to inheritance and adoption. In so doing, they sought to enforce the European Convention on Human Rights, which recognises families other than those based on the traditional marriage between a man and a woman. While the High Court ruled that a lesbian couple do not have the right to marry in Ireland under the Constitution (*Irish Times* 2006), national opinion polls reveal that there is increasing support for gay marriages in Ireland.

The constitutional understanding of the family – as consisting of children who live with their married parents and in a family situation where the mother is still based in the home – while still the official definition of the family in Ireland for legal purposes, is not the benchmark for family life in twenty-first century Ireland. The reality for many people is that, due to the escalating cost of home ownership, the family now includes grown-up children who are still living at home because of their inability to afford to buy or rent their own place.

Co-habitation, divorce and lone parenthood are also creating a new family-scape in Irish society. The number of divorced persons in Ireland has increased from 35,000 to 59,500 between 2002 and 2006 (Central Statistics Office (CSO) 2006). The number of separated (including divorced) persons increased from 87,800 in 1996 to 107,000 in 2006 (CSO 2006). Living arrangements are also changing, with the number of cohabiting couples up from 77,600 in 2002 to 121,800 in 2006 (CSO 2006). Lone parent families increased by about 23 per cent between 2002 and 2006 to almost 190,000 (CSO 2006). Falling fertility is having a significant impact on family size, with the average number of children per family declining from 2.2 in 1986 to 1.4 in 2006 (CSO 2006). The number of same sex couples has increased from 1,300 in 2002 to 2,090 in 2006 (CSO 2006). Marriage remains popular, with the number of marriages increasing by 110, 600 between 2002 and 2006 (CSO 2006). Accompanying these changes in family composition are major changes in the role and purposes of family life. The 'story' of family life is now part of a larger narrative on relationships and their place in fast-changing societies.

Democratisation of the Family

In order to gain a better understanding of contemporary family life, we need to think of family, not as a fixed structure, but rather as a set of values, activities and relationships which serve to meet the needs of adults and children. Anthony Giddens (1998) believes that what is now required of family is that it be responsive to changes in everyday life. Beck (1992) refers to this evolutionary process as the 'democratisation of the family'. The democratisation of the family is a reflexive process whereby changes in family dynamics have an influence on society and changes in society affect the way that families function. It may be helpful to think of family life as a particular social franchise for developing relationships which are capable of:

- promoting emotional and sexual equality;
- acknowledging mutual rights and responsibilities in relationships;
- facilitating co-parenting;
- accepting life-long parental contracts;
- negotiating authority with children;
- fulfilling obligations towards older family members.

To be successful, any franchised venture must appeal on some level to potential customers. Membership of a social franchise, such as the family, is more likely to be encouraged if individuals see the franchise as a operating on principles that are responsive to their needs. Challenges facing the new franchise include:

- Changing work practices – one's geographical location, employment status, range of skills and self identity are now open to change in the flexible new economy.
- Changes in intimate life – increased availability of birth control, visibility of gay and lesbian relationships, divorce and global development of feminism.

These changes in society have major consequences for the way that intimate adult relationships are patterned in day-to-day life at the beginning of the twenty-first century. The key features of these new-style relationships are that they are flexible, conditional and open to constant re-negotiation. Love lasts as long as it makes sense to each lover, just so long as they are both satisfied by the experience. Intimate relationships cannot be relied upon to provide adults with a platform for stability and they are open to constant negotiation and re-negotiation. Adults no longer feel obliged to follow socially sanctioned standards of commitment or to live out roles they have inherited from their parents. These changes in people's expectations for their relationships have played a major part in increasing divorce and co-habitation rates. They have also affected how children are parented. Destabilisation of adulthood in the sphere of intimate life has eroded the traditional basis of parents' authority over children. As flexibility has become a basic principle of intimate adult relationships, the reproduction of adult roles has become a less important feature of family life. Adults' status as 'experts' on how to live is cast into doubt. Children are now as actively involved as their parents in shaping their families through negotiation and participation in decision making.

We are witnessing the democratisation of the family, not only in Ireland, but in many different states across the globe. The international implications of this process for family-centred policy and practice development are generally positive: 'When family relations, both internal and external, are democratised and gender equitable, social capital will be developed, civil society will be promoted and democratic participation will improve' (Briar-Lawson *et al.* 2001: 17).

Submerged in social contexts that result in changed social practices and relations, adults have to come to terms with a growing uncertainty over the nature of childhood and a parallel uncertainty over suitable methods of dealing with children.

THE BEST INTERESTS OF THE CHILD

In all actions concerning children, whether undertaken by public or private social welfare institutions, courts of law, administrative authorities or legislative bodies, the best interests of the child shall be a primary consideration.
UN Convention on the Rights of the Child 1989, Article 3

Who decides on what constitutes the best interests of the child? With the emergence of children as global citizens – they are increasingly connected to a wider world through television, e-mail and the internet – their interests cut across the institutional boundaries of home and school. The UN Convention on the Rights of the Child was adopted by the General Assembly of the UN in 1989 and ratified by the Irish Government in 1992. Its 54 separate articles outline children's protection in the contexts of adoption, health, education and military service. All countries, save the USA and Somalia, have now ratified the Convention and, in so doing, have effectively promised to observe each of the 54 Articles.

Lee (2001) contends that the entire Convention and Article 12 in particular serves to generate what he terms positive 'childhood ambiguity'. He deems Article 12 to be ambivalent about children, as it contains a qualified provision for children's participation within the state's decision making process. Article 12 reads:

> State's Parties shall assure to the child who is capable of forming his or her own views the right to express those views freely in all matters affecting the child, the views of the child being given due weight in accordance with the age and maturity of the child. … The child shall in particular be provided the opportunity to be heard in any judicial and administrative proceedings affecting the child, either directly, or through a representative or an appropriate body, in a manner consistent with the procedural rules of natural law.

This ambivalence about a child's capability to have a voice of his or her own and about the level of attention that should be given to those voices is purposeful. The Convention's promises are carefully crafted so that they are applicable to all the world's children and the promises contained therein can be fulfilled by a very wide range of different responses to the matter of the child's voice. In this way, having generated positive childhood ambiguity, the Convention places the responsibility for managing that ambiguity on the legislatures and policy makers of the states that have ratified it. Lee (2001) contrasts the way in which this regulatory ambiguity is interpreted by the state with the ambiguity surrounding children's 'place' in contemporary Western society. As he points out:

> In the age of uncertainty, the weight of adult problems of maintaining social order has come to rest on poor children. Their ambiguity puts them in the position to be blamed for social problems and to be treated as a well-spring of social disorder. (69)

The reality of childhood for many Irish children from impoverished and socially excluded backgrounds is that, if their behaviour is deemed to pose a threat to legitimate social order, then it can be curbed and regulated through the use of a variety of sanctions, such as those contained in the Children Act 2001. Eoin O'Sullivan (2001) has stated that, despite government rhetoric claiming that the Act is offering a new approach to children deemed to be at risk of offending, there is little new in the Act.

The assorted family-based sanctions at the core of the Act hark back to the thinking behind the 1908 Children Act. In O'Sullivan's view, the provision of special care units, the introduction of curfews and pressurising parents to control their children (and sanctioning them if they fail to do

---

Blaming Children for Social Disorder in Ireland and the UK

Civil Rights Group Challenges Night Curfews for Teenagers

Night-time curfews, Labour's big idea to curb anti-social behaviour, will be challenged in the European Court of Human Rights after a teenager in West Sussex agreed to let the group Liberty bring a test case in his name. Under Section 30 of the Anti-Social Behaviour Act 2003, police have the power to pick up all children aged under sixteen who are outdoors after 9.00 p.m., regardless of their behaviour.

Officers take them to their homes and require them on pain of a fine or imprisonment to stay there until 6.00 a.m. The only way a child can be out after 9.00 p.m. is if they are accompanied by a responsible adult.

The Observer, 20 June 2004

Locking Children up is not the Key to Cutting Crime

The author of this article – Sean Redmond, a regional manager of the Barnardos Agency – questions the equation that more lock-up units and electronic tagging of children equals safer streets. Having looked at what is happening in the high support and special schools sector in Ireland he found that:

1. There is no consistent pattern of locking up children around the country.
2. Some regions proportionately lock up far less children than others.
3. Juvenile crime is no higher in these regions as a result of locking up less children; it could even be lower.

Irish Examiner, 19 May 2004

---

this) represents elements of a 'new conservatism' appealing to a nostalgic view of family and community. Goldson (2001) suggests that a symbolic 'demonisation of children' process instituted by the media around crime and wider social disorders paves the way for the institutional demonisation contained in the UK (Anti-Social Behaviour Act 2003) and Irish (Children Act 2001) Acts.

There is no doubt that the UN Convention, while providing a way forward, is only a framework and exerts a limited influence over national practices towards children. The UN Convention is not binding on individual states unless they incorporate it into national legislation and the only requirement which states must meet is to provide periodic reports to the UN Committee on the rights of the child. States are under moral rather than legal pressure to comply. Ireland has been censured by the Committee over its treatment of children from marginalised and excluded sections of Irish Society:

> With respect to the principle of non-discrimination (Article 2 of the UN Convention) the Committee is concerned by the disparities with regard to access to education and health services and notes the difficulties still faced by children from vulnerable and disadvantaged groups, including children belonging to the traveller community, children from poor families and refugee children as to the enjoyment of their fundamental rights, including access to education, housing and health services. (UN 1998, section 14)

While some change for the better has occurred in the eight years following the UN's condemnation of the Irish state's record on children's rights, the rate of change is disappointing. Table 2.1 sets out the state's record on children's rights to date.

A recent high profile 'tug-of-love' adoption case has generated public concern and placed pressure on the Government to improve the voice of children in legal proceedings affecting their welfare. The Government has now committed itself to holding a referendum on children's rights but the timing of such a referendum has yet to be announced.

A change in mind-set away from blaming children for social disorder and a move towards investment in community programmes, which will meet the needs of children and enable their parents to discharge their responsibilities in a productive and supportive fashion, is long overdue.

TABLE 2.1: STATE'S RECORD ON CHILDREN'S RIGHTS

Advances for Children:

- A minister for children who sits at the Cabinet table.
- A 10 year strategy to improve the lives of children has been adopted by the Government.
- Government spending on children's education and health has increased.
- An estimated 100,000 children have been lifted out of deprivation.
- An ombudsman for children has been appointed.

No Change:

- One in ten children lives in consistent poverty.
- Mental health services for children are grossly inadequate.
- Meagre supports and educational services for children with disabilities or developmental problems.
- A punitive and directionless youth justice system.
- No express recognition of children's rights in the Constitution. (Barnardos 2005)

Lost Ground:

- The disappearance of hundreds of separated children seeking asylum and the second rate treatment of children from refugee or asylum-seeking backgrounds who enter the state care system (*Irish Times* report, 29 October 2005).
- The introduction of ASBOs (anti-social behaviour orders) for children under 18 and over 12 in March 2007.

Key articles of the UN Convention on the Rights of the Child, which relate to children's participation, can be used to underpin community development and family support services relevant to new democratic family forms. Observing children's right to express opinions (Article 12), right to freedom of expression (Article 13), right to associate freely (Article 15), and right to play (Article 31) is a starting point for a broad reappraisal of the relationship between children, families and communities.

FAMILIES AS SOCIAL WELFARE ORGANISATIONS

While there may still be some truth in the saying of Miguel Cervantes' old grandmother – 'there are only two families in the world, the Haves and the Have-nots' – in contemporary Ireland, family structures, systems and dynamics vary. Despite their diversity Irish families – and indeed all families – share similar responsibilities and challenges. According to Cass and Cappo:

> Families are one of the most fundamental social networks: a major site of social and economic productive activity; the provider of intimacy and emotional interdependence for spouses/partners, parents, grandparents and children and other relatives; the provider of care, nurture and development of children and young people; and the provider of care for other family members made vulnerable by frailty associated with old age, by disability or severe illness …. Working life and family life, public life and private life are neither separate or separable. They are inextricably linked throughout the life course of both men and women, and for children and young people in ways which have significant implications for all public policies. (2005:14)

A number of factors have resulted in parents having less time and resources to devote to their own children and families. Changes in family structure that have been brought about by divorce, remarriage, co-habitation and lone parenthood; increasing participation of women in the labour force; increasing geographical mobility and excessive levels of social exclusion have left Irish families needing more support than ever. However, these changes have also left families and family members isolated, under increasing stress and less able to provide support for each other.

A Systems Theory Understanding of the Family

We can look at the family (in its broadest sense) from a systemic perspective, as a set of interrelating individuals and relationships, all of which affect and are affected by each other. This system is the context within which constituent members' needs may (or may not) be met. Certain tasks, such as those associated with childrearing, are undertaken by the family system. The family system operates within the wider social systems of the extended family, local community and society in which the family lives. Family tasks are affected by the surrounding social context and the degree of social integration between family members and their immediate environment. Miller and Bentovim (2003) have produced a model for rating family strengths and difficulties on family competence scales.

Their model is derived from family therapy theory and practice developed at the Great Ormond Street Hospital for Children in London. Within this model, factors affecting how families function can be grouped under the two headings of family organisation dimension and family character dimension.

Family Organisation Dimension

According to Miller and Bentovim:

> How families are organised is central to how well children's needs are met. This dimension includes the performance of a number of tasks and operations which are common to all families as part of organising everyday life, and important in bringing up children. So, for example, though families may have different ways of doing things, decision making and conflict resolution will be common to all. While there is an enormous range of parenting styles all children need stimulation, emotional warmth and encouragement if their development is to be promoted. (2003: 61)

Family organisation can be broken down further into the two component parts of family adaptability and parenting. Table 2.2 identifies the component parts of family organisation.

TABLE 2.2: FAMILY ADAPTABILITY AND PARENTING

Family Adaptability	Parenting
Organisational stability	Attachments
Decision making and problem solving	Guidance care and management of children
Relationships with the wider family and community	

The key elements of family adaptability are:

- Organisational adaptability – is concerned with a family's ability to adjust to and accommodate a diversity of roles, management of tasks, arrangements and responsibilities at different stages of the family life-cycle.

- Decision making and problem solving – who has power in the relationship and who has access to resources outside the family (such as income and social support). Cultural variations in the ways in which family members think about gender may affect the relative power of partners in decision making.
- Managing and resolving conflicts – acknowledging and responding to differences between members.
- Relationships with the wider family and community – the focus here is on the degree to which family members' relationships with the wider family and the community either help to meet the needs of family members or reduce their capacity to meet needs and thereby add to their difficulties.

The key elements of parenting are:

- Attachments – all children need close relationships of quality and character which positively connect them with significant carers in order to feel safe and secure.
- Guidance, care and management – parents' responsibility for care and protection and the setting of age appropriate realistic limits for children's behaviour.

Family Character Dimension

Each family has it's own particular *modus operandi* reflected through patterns of communication.

An Ecological Understanding of Families as Social Welfare Organisations

As well as using the systems perspective, we can look at the family from an ecological perspective, as set out by Jack and Gill (2003). Within the ecological perspective, the child, the child's family and the environments in which they live influence one another in a constant process of reciprocal interaction. The ecological understanding is 'borrowed' from biology and usually refers to the mutual interdependence of plants, animals, people and their physical environments. An ecological understanding is less concerned with the internal dynamics of families per se than the family systems model and is more focused on the ways in which these internal dynamics interact with the child's wider family, community and culture.

Quinton (2004), in his overview of the UK Supporting Parents Initiative, identifies the following points, the acknowledgement of which is central to the task of supporting parents in the community:

- In modern societies parenting is complex and hard to do.
- Parenting decisions arise from many influences.
- The ecological perspective points up the complexity between these influences and formal services are part of this ecology.
- All parents want to feel in control in dealing with parenting problems.
- Parents should first be seen as experts in their own parenting even when their views may need to be changed.
- Support is a relationship that requires respect and partnership.

Support is also a process – services need to get off on the right foot and be aware of and responsive to changing needs.

Supporting Families as Social Welfare Institutions

As this chapter has demonstrated, there is a precariousness about family life at the beginning of the twenty-first century. Interplay between the changing structure of families and the changing business of families is creating a new 'family-scape'. The process of democratisation of family relations requires shoring up internally and externally if the family as an institution is to rise to the challenge of looking after the best interests of children and acting as the primary social welfare organisation in society. Participants in the recent report *Families and Family Life in Ireland: Challenges for the Future* (Daly 2004) called on the Government to modernise its social systems and identified the following as core functions of a revamped and more developed family policy:

- support of and assistance with parenting;
- active involvement in the development and welfare of children;
- supporting active fatherhood;
- investing in family relations;
- investing in and supporting caring;
- reconciling family activities with the demands of modern life and changing Irish society.

Social capital, with its focus on social networks, participation and civic values can provide a useful framework for developing new policy and practice responses in family support work which are sympathetic to the core functions of a coherent and modern family policy.

CONCLUSION

Family support invites welfare professionals and local neighbourhood people to become custodians of a renewable asset – collective efficacy. Collective efficacy, or the capacity of a neighbourhood to implement its own plans, rests on the presence of a strong social capital – interconnected networks, trust among residents, social cohesion and a shared willingness to intervene for the common good. When residents and welfare professionals utilise collective efficacy to connect up neighbourhood facilities, neighbourhood processes and parents' perceptions of their neighbourhood, they are simultaneously harvesting and creating social capital. The next chapter highlights the strenuous efforts made by a family centre to sustain a commitment to this vision for services.

Chapter Three

A Family Support Story

Introduction

Social relations and networks represent intangible resources in people's lives that can either be nurtured or allowed to wither through neglect.

Gilchrist 2004: 121–122

In all family support activities the family is not seen as deficient but as having many strengths and resources. Dunst's (1995) family support principles draw our attention to different facets of human and social capital formation encompassed by a broad range of family-strengthening programmes:

1. Enhancing a sense of community.
2. Mobilising resources and supports.
3. Shared responsibility and collaboration.
4. Protecting family integrity.
5. Strengthening family functioning.
6. Proactive human service practices.

The family support story outlined in this chapter traces the evolution of a community-based family support centre and illustrates how centre-based family support, based on the six principles outlined above, increases the strengths of such communities by enhancing the capabilities of residents to enter into reciprocal exchanges, build trust and form social networks. The chapter also explores how these principles can be incorporated into activities and programmes which develop personal, social and economic capacities at a local level, thereby promoting not just parenting skills but broader fields of opportunity through social support networks which underpin people's capacity to care for each other. Put briefly, it is argued that the 'added value' of the approach taken by this particular family centre is that it integrates the task of human and social capital formation within a conceptual framework and practice repertoire which is broad, flexible and sufficiently robust to respond to the needs of individual agents, the relationships between them and the networks they form. This account of the centre's development draws upon Fitzgerald's 2004 study of the centre covering the period 1984–2004. The chapter then focuses on an evaluation of the experiences of the centre's stakeholders. Users of the centre, along with staff, management committee members and external stakeholders were interviewed as part of the evaluation and their views are presented in the final section of the chapter. Aspects of the family support centre addressed in this chapter include:

- Historical development of the family centre.
- Service delivery framework.
- An evaluation of the centre.
- Family support and community development.

The Particularity of Neighbourhood Circumstances

While not explicitly identified, no attempt is made to make anonymous the location of the family support centre detailed in this chapter. As suggested by Warr (2005):

> When particular places are singled out to be explored in research, the details of place as they feature in the accounts of the people who live there are critical contexts for understanding. The places where people live comprise complex layers of experience and meaning which have historical, social and demographic specificity. In order to preserve the richness of details it is arguably theoretically undesirable, if not practically difficult, to anonymise such places for the purpose of research (Nespoor 2000). Anonymisation involves stripping away distinctive features of a place lest they identify a town,

but this raises other problems for research explicitly concerned with particular places as contexts for the experiences of the people who live there. (8–9)

HISTORICAL DEVELOPMENT OF THE CENTRE

'It was a life line, as they say; you are never prepared for being a parent.'

This comment was made during an interview with a young parent who found herself living on a new housing estate (built in 1982) on the edge of an Irish provincial town in the early 1980s. All of the residents were young and there was an immediate need for pre-schools and early intervention services. The local health board (statutory health and personal social services provider) responded to the needs of this new neighbourhood by providing funding for a community playgroup. A community worker working in the health board at that time remembers that the coming on-stream of small grants for funding community playgroups marked a new departure in the work of health board community workers. Hitherto their work had been focused on the needs of the elderly. A group of women with young children from the estate approached the health board and another community worker responded by securing funding for a playgroup which commenced in 1984 in a temporary building. The community playgroup was the focal point for further community initiatives such as adult education classes provided by the local authority's vocational education committee. Volunteers and service users became involved in community development work (on the playgroup or management committee and in the growing range of services) and the role of the management committee itself evolved over time.

The early work of those involved with the playgroup, and the increasing number of activities associated with it, contributed to a growing interpersonal economy in the neighbourhood. An interpersonal economy fosters skills, competences, capacities and connections and leads to the establishment of social networks. By drawing on this interpersonal economy, over time the centre addressed issues of respect and belonging and helped to lubricate the transition of people from the positions of new entrants to the neighbourhood to fully fledged members of a dynamic community.

The networks in turn helped to 'bed down' the neighbourhood by allowing for the development of social norms – generally unwritten but commonly understood ways of behaving that are valued or socially approved. Social norms are forms of informal social control which remove the need for more formal institutionalised legal sanctions or garda (police) presence in communities. Where social capital is high there tends to be a reduced rate of crime and less need for formal policing.

By 1988–89 the activities linked to the playgroup had expanded and included disco dancing, women's groups, light entertainment, various parades and youth groups. New estates were being constructed in surrounding areas ('R—' (1986) – 90 houses and 'G—' (1991) – 117 houses) and these families were also using the facilities. According to a project leader, interviewed in 2002:

> We were also very aware of the need for crèche facilities. Parents also identified this need.

The centre was catering for approximately 150 families when it was decided to move it to a new purpose-built structure which would allow for further expansion to take place. The same project leader explained how this came about:

> The Urban District Council donated land and also drew up the plans for the building. Funding for the project came from the health board, People in Need, Combat Poverty, the Urban District Council, St. Vincent de Paul, Lions Club, the Parish and local businesses. The support and advice came from FÁS [government employment agency], the health board and the urban district council. A FÁS community youth training programme built the centre. This meant that we paid for materials. FÁS paid the foreman and craftsmen; and early school leavers had the opportunity to learn new skills from the experts. In November 1991 the Family Resource Centre was officially opened by the President.

The construction of a purpose-built centre extended the sphere of operations of the newly-formed management committee. Workers on community employment schemes supplemented the work of volunteers in some services and simultaneously allowed for the introduction of entirely new services. The range of services now included crèche facilities, environmental projects, extended pre-school services, youth groups, care-taking, administrative support and adult education.

Membership of the management committee at this point in time included service users, parish representatives, individuals with particularly useful skills or expertise, health board representatives and community representatives.

Further construction ('C—C—' (1995) – 49 houses and 'M—' (1998) – 36 houses) in the surrounding area intensified the demand for services and led to the further expansion of the centre. In 1999, FÁS – through its Community Youth Training programme – commenced the work on land donated by the urban district council. The centre was also granted family resource centre status by the Department of Social, Community and Family Affairs (now the Department of Social and Family Affairs) around this time and this allowed for the appointment of a project co-ordinator. It also placed the centre's funding on a more secure level.

An application for funding to increase staffing was submitted to a childcare manager in the health board and the health board's family support committee towards the end of 2000. The application was successful and the following four full-time staff were employed:

- pre-school co-ordinator;
- community childcare worker for children aged six to twelve;
- out-reach worker for the twelve- to twenty-year-olds;
- administrator.

In 2001, membership of the management committee was expanded and was drawn from:

- area representation;
- service users;
- people involved in programmes or projects;
- people involved in women's groups;
- representatives from youth activities groups;
- representatives from sports events;
- staff representatives;
- residents' associations;
- other agencies involved in delivering services (e.g. local health board).

Table 3.1 sets out the development of centre services from 1984–2007 and Table 3.2 provides a centre timetable.

TABLE 3.1: FAMILY CENTRE SERVICE DEVELOPMENT

Services that Developed between 1984 and 1991

    Playgroup: initial service

    Mother and toddler group

    Residents' association

    Women's group

    Adult education

    Arts and crafts

    Halloween and Christmas party

    Children's games

    Community games

    Drama classes

    Judo

    Soccer clubs

    Irish dancing

    Summer camps

    Playground

    Baton twirling

Services that Developed between 1991 and 2000

    Community employment schemes

    Folk choir group

    Summer scheme

    Credit union

    Health services

    Garda soccer league

    Fun days

    Learning is fun club

    St. Patrick's day parades

    Music lessons

Continued …

Services that Developed between 2001 and 2007

Day trips

Out of school hours programme (for children aged 6–12 years)

Homework and activity clubs

Senior drama group

Adult literacy group

Outreach services (for young people aged 12–21 years)

Senior youth group

Parenting course

Pathfinders

Junior youth leader award

Drop-in centre

Sports access projects

Sports coaching awards

Basketball project

Indoor football programme

Community arts project

Band project

Youth computer classes

Young women's groups

Adult education

Community day out

Organic garden

Arts club

Women's group and senior citizens' group

English and Irish classes

Rapid Readers programme

Childcare training and parenting courses

TABLE 3.2: FAMILY CENTRE SERVICES ON OFFER IN 2003

	Monday	Tuesday	Wednesday	Thursday	Friday
8.30 a.m.–9.30 a.m.	Peter Pan Crèche	Peter Pan Crèche	Peter Pan Crèche	Peter Pan Crèche	Peter Pan Crèche
9.30 a.m.–11.30 a.m.	1. Peter Pan Crèche 2. Playgroup 3. Computer Course	1. Peter Pan Crèche 2. Playgroup 3. Computer Course	1. Peter Pan Crèche 2. Playgroup 3. Computer Course	1. Peter Pan Crèche 2. Playgroup 3. Computer Course	1. Peter Pan Crèche 2. Playgroup 3. Computer Course
11.30 a.m.–12.30 a.m.	1. Peter Pan Crèche 2. Computer Course	1. Peter Pan Crèche 2. Computer Course	1. Peter Pan Crèche 2. Computer Course	1. Peter Pan Crèche 2. Computer Course	1. Peter Pan Crèche 2. Computer Course
12.30 p.m.–1.30 p.m.	1. Peter Pan Crèche 2. Playgroup 3. Computer Course	1. Peter Pan Crèche 2. Playgroup 3. Computer Course	1. Peter Pan Crèche 2. Playgroup 3. Computer Course	1. Peter Pan Crèche 2. Playgroup 3. Computer Course	1. Peter Pan Crèche 2. Playgroup 3. Computer Course
1.30 p.m.–2.30 p.m.	1. Peter Pan Crèche 2. Playgroup	1. Peter Pan Crèche 2. Playgroup	1. Peter Pan Crèche 2. Playgroup	1. Peter Pan Crèche 2. Playgroup	1. Peter Pan Crèche 2. Playgroup

Continued …

	Monday	Tuesday	Wednesday	Thursday	Friday
2.30 p.m.–3.30 p.m.	1. Peter Pan Crèche 2. Computer Course	1. Peter Pan Crèche 2. Computer Course	1. Peter Pan Crèche 2. Computer Course	1. Peter Pan Crèche 2. Computer Course	1. Peter Pan Crèche 2. Computer Course
3.30 p.m.–4.30 p.m.	1. Peter Pan Crèche 2. Homework Club 3. Computer Course	1. Peter Pan Crèche 2. Homework Club 3. Computer Course	1. Peter Pan Crèche 2. Homework Club 3. Computer Course	1. Peter Pan Crèche 2. Homework Club 3. Computer Course	1. Peter Pan Crèche 2. Homework Club 3. Computer Course
4.30 p.m.–5.30 p.m.	1. Homework Club 2. Drop-in Centre (5–6 p.m.)	Music Classes	Homework Club	Homework Club	Drop-in Centre
5.30 p.m.–6.30 p.m.		1. Senior Drama 2. Music Classes	Drop-in Centre	1. French 2. Thursday Group (6 p.m.)	Activity Club
6.30 p.m.–7.30 p.m.	RS Group	Dance Classes		Thursday Group	
7.30 p.m.–8.30 p.m.	Youth Group (7.30 p.m. – 9.00 p.m.)	Tai-Chai	Computer Classes	Thursday Group	
8.30 p.m.–9.30 p.m.			Computer Classes		

A PRODUCTIVE SERVICE DELIVERY FRAMEWORK

From its earliest days right up until the present, the centre has been firmly based within a community development framework rather than a 'crisis-oriented' model of intervention offering 'therapeutic' help to children and families in need. The centre offered practical responses to locally defined need. Fitzgerald notes:

> The people of the community identified a need for services within their community in the 1980s and they themselves took action leading to many resources, classes, activities and groups being organised locally. At this time the centre and the groups were totally dependant on volunteers. (2004: 9)

Similarly, the principles of open access, self-referral and user participation were fundamental to the approach adopted by the volunteers who gave up their time to enhance and provide services to all in the community. These 'natural helpers' were concerned with providing 'better beginnings' for children and 'new opportunities' for adults. Residents were willing to volunteer for tasks which demonstrated a commitment both to individual self-interest and the public interest. A great deal of fundraising was required to overcome the lack of tangible resources available to the community. However, involvement in family centre activities was having a 'multiplier effect' on resource levels available to the community as a whole. Initially, residents were drawn to the centre in order to meet people and gain a sense of belonging. Self-help and community building operated as a collective mechanism for sharing risks and resources in the circumstances of scarcity and insecurity which confronted new residents of the housing development. The sum of bonding social capital available to residents was boosted by the emergence of community networks based around the playgroup and the increasing number of activities associated with it, including adult education, Irish dancing, judo, summer camps and drama classes. Learning some of the rough and tumble of group processes helped to interconnect residents and created space for chat, trust and warmth to grow. These interconnections solidified into networks characterised by:

- High levels of reciprocity – a resident provides a service to others or acts for the benefit of others at a personal cost. They do this with the general expectation that this kindness will be returned at some undefined time in the future when they might need it themselves. In a community where reciprocity is strong, people care for each other's interests.
- Trust – entails a willingness to take risks in a social situation. Residents act in this way because they are confident that others will respond as expected and will act in mutually supportive ways or at least that others do not intend harm.

Linking social capital was derived from the positive association between the family centre and the local community work department operating under the aegis of the statutory health and personal social services provider. According to Fitzgerald:

The Community Work Department from the Southern Health Board supported the management committee which was made up of representatives from the community. They offered support and guidance and assisted the group to plan strategically. The Community Work department was also integral in the provision of grant aid from within the Health Board, and in supporting the group and assisting them in making funding applications to other organisations. The Community Work Department were involved in all aspects of the centre's development, from attending meetings to supporting the management in their own development. (2004: 9)

Establishing Community Networks

Gilchrist (2004) sets out the benefits of community and social networks:

- They provide an alternative user-friendly source of help during crisis points for those seeking help with risky or embarrassing problems who do not wish to resort to professional (sometimes stigmatised) service provision.
- Social networks supply informal care over and above the care provided by family and friends.

- In addition to these practical benefits, social networks provide their members with opportunities for positive emotional engagement:

  Social psychologists have studied happiness and conclude that social interaction of almost any kind tends to make people happy, both in the short term but also in terms of their general disposition (Argyle 1989). It appears that it is not only the quality of social interaction that has this effect but also the quantity. People with diverse networks (maintained through a variety of activities) seem to exist on a higher level of contentment than those with an intensely supportive, but homogenous set of relationships (Argyle 1996a, 1996b; Ornish 1999). This also applies to reported levels of health in that individuals with robust and diverse networks lead healthier lives than those who are more isolated or whose networks consist of similar people (Flynn 1989; Yen and Syme 1999). (2004: 8)

- Community networks foster informal modes of communication and co-operation between people.
- Community networks underpin collective action strategies which are focused on people working together to achieve or defend shared interests.

EVALUATING THE CENTRE

The centre was evaluated in 2003. The focus of the evaluation, which was commissioned by the Health Board's Community Work Department, was on:

- the historical development of the centre;
- service operation;
- the future of the centre.

A formative evaluation strategy (assessing the processes involved) allowed for the adoption of a dialogical approach to the research. This approach is inclusive insofar as its goal is to produce input to the ongoing social dialogue and praxis in society, rather than attempting to generate ultimate, unequivocally verified knowledge. By gaining an understanding of processes, it becomes possible to see which elements are contributing to the assessed results or not and the extent to which a service is actually being provided in a way which corresponds with official plans or accounts. As Miller *et al.* put it:

> What are known as stakeholder or participatory approaches aim to mitigate the negative implications associated with more traditional approaches to evaluation. Actively engaging multiple stakeholders results in agreement on what is to be evaluated, how the evaluation will be conducted and who will benefit as a result. The content and form of the evaluation process are therefore generated by the interests and needs of the stakeholders (Mathie and Greene 1997) ... evaluation must accommodate the equally valid interpretations of all stakeholders of the nature and value of a project. (2002: 22–23)

The rationale for the stakeholder participatory approach to evaluation which was utilised throughout the research project is twofold:

- Accountability – the principle that all organisations, including community-led organisations, are duty bound to be accountable and be strategically aware of the impact which they are having on their stakeholders and society in general.
- Learning – 'Learning is also an important rationale for monitoring and evaluation. Organisations, like individuals, need to learn from their experience if they are to grow and develop. Without monitoring and evaluation an organisation will not be able to reflect on the appropriateness of the means or the ends that constitute the essence of its work.' (McKeown 1999: 53)

Using information gathered from interviews, the next section explores the perspective of the centre's management committee.

Evaluating the Centre – Interviews with the Family Centre Management Committee

Question One – What are the Strategic Aims and Objectives of the Centre?

The aim is to provide services that are identified – through a community development process – as being necessary or desirable for the advancement of the communities and catchment areas served by the centre. In practice, no request for a service or facility has thus far been refused. Operationally, the purpose of the centre is to create access to services bringing in employment and training. Access to employment is facilitated through the crèche. The broader aim of the centre is to become the focal point for a process which will assist the greater integration of communities. Education is the key factor in this overall process. Centre users are often individuals who may have missed out on educational opportunities.

Question Two – What is the Role of the Management Committee in Realising these Aims and Objectives?

The management committee is responsible for discharging operational tasks such as accessing and securing funding for service development, trying to work within a budget, developing services and expanding the centre (e.g. through the building of an extension). Because the centre receives its funding from a variety of sources and different statutory organisations, there is a great deal of tension associated with funding tasks. A committee member's comment during an interview puts this 'tension' in context: 'In an ideal world one source of funding would be helpful. However we don't get preoccupied by finances.' On the developmental side, the committee is responsible for listening to the people who come into the centre and responding to the needs of service users. The following comment from a committee member shows how a culture of involvement between the centre and its users is promoted: 'The importance of having an open door policy comes to the fore here. As a board of management we have a big commitment there – to get the feedback.' Staff development, training and support is another major responsibility of the committee.

Three sub-groups have been established to make better use of limited resources and time – staff support, finance and development. The committee have to adopt a pragmatic attitude in order to keep the show on the road, as the following remark from a committee member interviewed makes clear:

> Just to put things in perspective, we are all acutely aware of the economic climate that's here at the moment. We are not in a position to look too far down the road. We are constantly planning from year to year. The planning is affected by these pressures and more strategic long-term planning would be preferable.

Question Three – What Contribution do the Various Stakeholders make to Realising these Aims and Objectives?

External stakeholders contribute advice and a lot of support to the centre through their networking activities (attending committees and sub-committees of organisations and agencies which can help the centre in different ways).

Members of the management committee are also involved in outside committee work and are in a position to network with external stakeholders. Outside stakeholders do not interfere or intrude upon the work of the centre. They have no agendas and realise that the building is owned by the community. They have brought services such as the Vocational Educational Committee (VEC) and FÁS to the community.

Internal stakeholders contribute experiences, expertise, skills, creativity, commitment and enthusiasm. All the staff are committed to the following mission statement of the centre:

> The management committee aspire to improving the quality of life of all people living in our area. We believe that, by working in an inclusive and empowering way, all individuals will be in a better position to participate socially, economically and culturally in society. Through the Community Employment project, the pre-school provision, youth groups, local residents groups and the Estate Enhancement programme and working in close co-operation with FÁS, Southern Health Board, Tralee Urban District Council, gardaí, Kerry Education Services, Department of Social and Family Affairs, Kerry Dioscesan Youth Service, Partnership Trá Lí and other local voluntary groups, we hope to achieve our aim of full participation by all.

There is a difference between working as a childcare worker in a community capacity and working as a childcare worker in a private capacity. As one committee member interviewed put it: 'It's an inbuilt thing once people come in the door here to work; once you come in the door you buy into a team. The mission and ethos means that people approach the thing with a particular attitude rather than just providing a service, a task, and being here to take your wages and walk out the door kind of thing.'

Question Four – What are the Strengths of the Centre?

In a sense one of the strengths is the self-interest involved. The centre promotes mutuality because it is directly concerned with the community. This was summed up by one committee member:

> When you work in a community you are putting something in and at the same time you are getting something back – you are working with your own people you know. Being a contributor, not just a receiver. The open-door policy is a big strength here. The centre is accessible – user friendly and within walking distance of everybody. It is in the centre of a big catchment area.

Question Five – What are the Weaknesses of the Centre?

The uncertainty attached to funding is a big weakness because, despite having a three-year work plan, the centre operates from year to year without the security of guaranteed funding. The centre is dependent on the Community Employment scheme and could not maintain delivery of services without it. Another weakness from the centre's point of view is that when trained, community employment workers may move on to employment outside the centre.

Question Six – What are the Opportunities for Further Development of the Centre?

Services for the elderly need to be developed. More needs to be done around improving educational opportunities. Outreach work and further community development are areas which need to be expanded, particularly in light of the continuing growth in a population that may wish to access the services that the centre provides. However management must also bear in mind that over-development can serve to reduce the quality of services on offer. As one committee member interviewed cautioned:

> You can spread your wings too far and become anonymous. It is for management to review as we go along. We are developing ourselves. I suppose this goes back to the three-year plan. Are we going to be able to facilitate all the people who will be living in the 200 new houses between here and R—? Well, that will be open for discussion.

We are a growing community and childcare and other needs are growing all the time.

Question Seven – What are the Threats to further Development?

- Over-development of the service and loss of quality and the personal touch as a result.
- Inadequate or insecure funding.
- The curtailment of the Community Employment scheme.
- Threats to the funding of external stakeholders.
- Families and individuals leaving the area.

Evaluating the Centre – Focus Group Interview with the Centre's Staff

Staff members who participated in the group were: a community employment supervisor, a childcare and crèche worker, an administrator, a pre-school co-ordinator, an outreach worker (12–21 year olds) and a community childcare worker.

The centre provides a starting point for personal development for a lot of people. A person might begin by bringing a child to the crèche and then see a notice about an adult education class that interests them. There is an opportunity for children to maintain and develop progressive relationships through involvement in the centre – 'We have found in general that children who start in the crèche and move on to the pre-school tend to move on to the after school clubs and the youth clubs and keep involved over the years. It has to be good for them. We have had teenagers here on work experience who actually went to the pre-school when they were three.' Mothers have childcare facilities available to them and they can take up training opportunities and part-time or full-time work.

The centre fosters the growth of trust so that positive work can be accomplished for and on behalf of residents: 'A lot of the parents build up trusting relationships with you and, if they need to be referred to housing, you can set that up. They trust you enough to tell you that you could do that for them.'

This trust is based on the principle of confidentiality which is very important to how the centre works. Parents might need other supports and they may not always be aware of what they need. The staff can offer advice on the options available to them. For example, parents might need a subsidy to help with childcare costs and they may not be aware that the health board can subsidise these costs. The centre provides a range of services for children:

> The social side of children is developed by building up trusting relationships between the children and the adults who work with them. Again, the continuity is important – children progress from crèche to playgroup. Children using these services are provided with breakfast at 10.00 a.m. and lunch at 12.15 p.m. Food is a basic need. They get a full, hot meal at lunchtimes and it might be the only hot meal that some children get in the day … . They love going in the kitchen. Do they try and help you? They do–they are not allowed but they do! We know what each child likes at this stage and their allergies.

Everyone in the centre has a role in making people in the community aware of what is going on in the centre. Charges for any of the services are so minimal that everything is affordable for most people. However, if somebody had an urgent or pressing need, then we would target them for a service on an informal basis.

Evaluating the Centre – Interviews with External Stakeholders

A number of significant external stakeholders were identified by the centre's project leader. Five interviews were held in May 2003. Each stakeholder was asked to discuss their experiences of the centre and to address the following three questions:

1. What has been achieved?
2. What is being achieved?
3. What could be achieved?

Interview with Probation and Welfare Officer, 7 May 2003

What has been achieved?
The family resource centre is a valuable community resource. It now constitutes a focal point in the community for young people. Probation and Welfare clients benefit from the facilities and services which are provided there. The local area does not have a high profile in terms of

offending behaviours and the centre has been influential here. Probation and Welfare and the centre have collaborated in developing a diversionary programme. There are no glaring gaps in the services provided at the centre. The building is of a very high standard and this gives out a positive message about the programmes being run there.

What is being achieved?
An appreciation of the value of people. We don't know enough about the impact that some programmes have on people. However, the probation officer is aware of one person whose offending behaviour went way down as a result of their attending the music programme. It is providing good services for teenagers.

What could be achieved?
There should be a family resource centre in each community, which is not reliant on volunteers but is professionally run.

Interview with General Services Manager, Southern Health Board, 9 May 2003

What has been achieved?
Partnership has been achieved. Experience has taught the manager that a lack of social infrastructure and bad planning can be held responsible for poor social outcomes. This is a major issue when it comes to the provision of public housing. Social exclusion can result in negative health outcomes. The family centre exists because twenty years ago local people approached the Southern Health Board and looked for services. Over the intervening twenty years it has grown and become an excellent resource.

What is being achieved?
The focus of the centre is on health and well-being. The social benefit of the centre is manifested through improved health outcomes for the community. There is good interdisciplinary support and public involvement in the project. The biggest input of the Health Board is the involvement of significant professionals such as the community work department, social workers and community welfare officers in the development and day-to-day running of the centre. These professionals have prioritised and responded to the needs of the area. A measure of the success of the

centre is that people from the area are now going on to third-level education. The centre offers the Health Board an opportunity to be involved in service delivery which is working pro-actively with individuals at a pre-school level.

What could be achieved?

The centre constitutes an example of what the Health Board does well. It should be replicated in other areas. It provides us with a model. There are good examples of community-based services for the elderly operating in other areas which can be used as a model. Services for the elderly is an area where development of this model could achieve a great deal.

The Health Board can provide expertise and professionalism for these kind of programmes. Whatever kind of centre develops, it needs to be robust enough to respond to the changing needs of society.

Interview with Community Guard, 12 May 2003

What has been achieved?

The centre provided me with a significant opportunity to get to know the community. I got to know all the local people who were actively involved in the family centre. Prior to going up there I was part of a team, but the centre became my 'team' once I began to get involved in the activities and programmes it supported. It is too soon to show results in terms of reducing offending levels. The Southern Health Board has been helpful in funding the centre but a great deal of the service or programme development work fell back on the management committee. The Southern Health Board community worker and the project leader were very helpful.

What is being achieved ?

The community guard has been on the board of management for a number of years and witnessed the transformation in people who come onto the board. The music project, which he piloted, is now a mainstream programme under the Vocational Education Committee (VEC).

What could be achieved ?

It is too soon to show results in terms of a reduction in offending behaviours. However, greater targeting of high-risk potential offenders could show results. The majority of families just go about their business, rely on their own resources and access the services available in the centre. There is a need, however, to concentrate resources on disadvantaged families – families with poor social skills who may have some difficulty using the centre fully. There is a cluster of such families who need specific targeting. The criminal law is totally ineffective in dealing with social problems and may exacerbate financial problems.

Interview with Social Worker, 22 May 2003

Since the Southern Health board social work department does not cover the centre's catchment area on a 'patch' basis, no one social worker has responsibility for the catchment area. As a result, the social worker has had limited contact with the centre. Based on her experiences in working with the centre she commented that staff in the centre dealing with children with behavioural problems should have more training. She also felt that the staff in the centre required more resources to enable them to work with children with particular difficulties.

Interview with the Public Health Nurse, 28 May 2003

The public health nurse commenced working in the area in September 2002. The area is split and another public health nurse covers R—. The public health nurse wants to use the centre for clinics. She feels that a clinic in the centre, rather than in town, would facilitate parents in the area. Such a clinic would have a child welfare focus and a 'drop in' approach, which would serve to empower parents.

Evaluating the Centre – Users' Perceptions of the Centre

Questionnaires were distributed to a random sample of service users drawn from the different programmes provided by the centre. There were five male and twenty female respondents. Most of the users surveyed fall into the following categories – female, aged 36 or less, with children under twelve years and using services for over one to two years. The questionnaires revealed the users' experiences of the centre under the following headings.

Quality of Services

The term 'quality' is used to refer to the way in which the centre's services are experienced by users. This experience is measured by asking respondents for their level of agreement or disagreement with six key statements:

1. I was made to feel welcome at the centre.
2. I enjoy coming to the centre.
3. The centre gives me help when I need it.
4. I get good advice at the centre.
5. The centre is always there to support me.
6. When I have something to say about services I am encouraged to speak my mind.

The results of the survey indicate that virtually every user had a very positive experience of the centre. The most frequent response (80–90 per cent) to each statement was that it was 'always true' or 'often true'. The centre is regarded and experienced as an excellent service.

Personal, Family and Community Impacts of the Family Centre

Again respondents were invited to register agreement or disagreement with the following key statements about the centre:

1. The centre has been a big help to me.
2. The centre has been a big help to my family.
3. The centre has been a big help to the community.

Respondents unequivocally (100 per cent) agreed that the centre has been a big help to the community. Seventy-three per cent of respondents agreed that the centre has always been a big help to them and 81 per cent said that the centre has always been a big help to their families.

The direct impact of the centre on users was also measured. In total, between 80 per cent and 90 per cent of respondents either stated that: 'by using the centre I have greatly improved my life' (50 per cent); or 'life is much better since I began using the centre' (38.5 per cent). Only one respondent recorded no positive change in their life since they began attending the centre.

The Centre's Profile in the Area

The results indicate that there is 100 per cent agreement 'that the centre is needed in the area'. Ninety-two per cent indicated that the statement 'the centre is appreciated in the area' is always true. Sixty-five per cent felt that 'most people know what is happening in the centre' is always a true statement.

Activities Participated in at the Centre

Findings here make it clear that users participate in a 'spread' of activities encompassing personal development work, skills and educational development, recreation and leisure programmes.

Qualities of the Centre's Staff

Eighty-eight per cent to 90 per cent of respondents believe that the following statements are always true:

- Staff in the centre genuinely care about you.
- Staff in the centre know how to respect people.
- Staff in the centre are fair.
- Staff in the centre are very good at what they do.

Least Helpful Aspect of the Centre

Overall, respondents made little or no negative comments about the centre. There was a plea for more clubs, activities and services for children and more flexibility around the scheduling of education and training courses.

FAMILY SUPPORT AND COMMUNITY DEVELOPMENT

According to Twelvetrees:

> Some needs can be met from the resources existing within the community or at least with limited support from outside the community. Social events, play-schemes, youth clubs, lunch clubs for older people, voluntary visiting schemes, Alcoholic Anonymous groups, some educational classes, even in certain situations the building of a

community centre and some aspects of job creation would all come into this category. In these types of situations the group is involved in a 'service' strategy using primarily the resources of the community (though it can also be seen as a self-help strategy). (1991: 8)

The origins of the family resource centre described in this chapter are to be found in a service strategy pursued through a community development process. Although family support policy is now very much a part of public discourse, a key question for any discussion of family support must be: what is the need which is involved? On a very broad level, Mill's (1969) distinction for addressing questions about individual and family needs – personal troubles are different from social issues – is the core conceptual focus of two different policy frames. A categorical approach to policies (Briar-Lawson *et al.* 2001) and practices exists when families are viewed separately and in isolation from other needs and priorities. Policy makers' attention is focused on categories of individuals, e.g. children or women or older people. Families are seen as just one of many sectors or categories in society competing for services.

A relational approach to family policies and practices is based on an understanding of the responsibilities, meaning and significance of families and their contribution to the societal culture. The interrelationships between families, other social institutions (e.g. schools) and other policy categories (e.g. economics) are prioritised. Family support that lacks this wider relational vision has a static as opposed to a dynamic nature.

McGrath, in his 2003 study of the Western Health Board (now HSE) family support projects and the Department of Community, Rural and Gaeltacht Affairs community development projects, found that few opportunities for closer integration between family support and community development principles and practices existed: 'While family support in general need not necessarily entail community involvement, community development cannot be reasonably viewed in isolation from supporting families and young people'(McGrath 2003).

CONCLUSION

This chapter has chronicled the key elements and tactics employed in an evolving family support project with a commitment to collective ways of addressing problems. The project does not just provide family support but enables people acting on their own behalf to support each other. In this way it avoids the risk of stigma as described in a small scale study of service users' experiences of family support services. According to Jackson and Heffernan:

> Health professionals may view family support services as being beneficial but the women saw an attached stigma if they used the services. The interviewees acknowledged that they needed help with their childrearing but using family support services was perceived to be a proclamation of bad motherhood. It was suggested to the interviewees that family support services were not a 'cure' for inadequate parenting but were modern society's answer to the disappearing extended family network. The interviewees did not agree with this. Family support services were seen as an admission of irresponsibility. (2004: 39)

A community development approach, aimed at developing natural helping networks around families and generating social capital at the neighbourhood level, avoids the risk of stigma being attached to service users. The next chapters build on this discussion through an exploration of international programmes that support families and create social capital.

CHAPTER FOUR

STORIES FROM ABROAD

INTRODUCTION

This chapter explores the policy and practice contexts within which family support programmes in the UK and Australia have been operating and evolving over the course of the last thirty years or so, up until the time of writing in 2007. It highlights some of the challenges facing policy makers and practitioners attempting to operationalise family support aims and values and shows how solutions can cross countries. More specifically, it is argued that there is much to be gained from collaboration across countries to develop knowledge and skills that can be employed to promote the well-being of children, families and their communities.

Though they may have developed different versions of well-being, both the UK and Australia aspire to place family support at the top of their current welfare agendas. Broadly speaking, both countries are actively involved in commissioning community development programmes which seek to promote generalised social cohesion and positive social functioning for families. It is therefore useful to examine the range of approaches adopted by both countries to family support in order to begin to explore the effectiveness of specific intervention strategies.
Areas addressed in this chapter include:

- The Australian family support and capacity building system.
- Supporting families in the UK – the relationship between the Children Act 1989, *Every Child Matters* (2003) and the Children Act 2004.

THE AUSTRALIAN FAMILY SUPPORT AND CAPACITY BUILDING SYSTEM

Overview

A variety of approaches to family support and wider community development have emerged in Australia. In addition to Australian indigenous programmes, models have also been introduced into Australia the origins of which lie in the UK or the US. According to Scott:

> Over the past decade we have seen a growth in imported family strengthening models from the United Kingdom and the United States. These include secondary prevention programs such as volunteer-based home visiting services like Homestart (introduced by the Family Action Centre, University of Newcastle) and tertiary prevention programs like Newpin, a group therapy and non-residential therapeutic community program for depressed mothers introduced by Burnside, a non-government child and family welfare organisation in Sydney. (2001: 6–7)

The family-centred approaches adopted by these programmes are rooted in the ecological conception of the family as the primary resource for a child's well-being. This ecological understanding of families and communities developed by Bronfenbrenner (1979) and Germain (1979) provides us with an analytical tool for examining the connection between community development, family support and social capital. In Australia, Eva Cox generated considerable discussion of social capital through her 1995 Boyer Lectures. In the Boyer Lectures, she said:

> There are four major capital measures, one of which takes up far too much policy time and space at present. This is financial capital. Physical capital makes it onto the agenda because of the environmental movement. So there are fierce debates on trees, water, coal and what constitutes sustainable development. Some types of physical capital and financial capital deplete with overuse, or become scarce or too expensive. We occasionally mention human capital – the total of our skills and knowledge – but rarely count its loss in unemployment.
> There has been too little attention paid to social capital.... Social capital refers to the processes between people which establish

networks, norms, social trust and facilitate co-ordination and co-op-eration for mutual benefit. These processes are also known as social fabric or glue, but I am deliberately using the term 'capital' because it invests the concept with the reflected status from other forms of capital. Social capital is also appropriate because it can be measured and quantified so we can distribute its benefits and avoid its losses.

We increase social capital by working together voluntarily in egalitarian organisations. Learning some of the rough and tumble of group processes also has the advantages of connecting us with others. We gossip, relate and create the warmth that comes from trusting. Accumulated social trust allows groups and organisations, and even nations, to develop the tolerance sometimes needed to deal with conflicts and differing interests.

Social capital should be the pre-eminent and most valued form of any capital as it provides the basis on which we build a truly civil society. Without our social bases we cannot be fully human. Social capital is as vital as language for human society. (Australian Broadcasting Corporation)

Social capital has been identified by the Commonwealth Department of Family and Community Services (2000) as a key element of its community building strategy. Many state and territory governments have also acknowledged the importance of social capital as a resource which can make a positive contribution to community-based family support projects.

Family Support History in Australia

The need for family support services was identified and publicly de-bated in the late 1960s and early 1970s. In 1978, the Commonwealth Government's Office of Child Care piloted the Family Support Services Scheme. Its purpose was 'to assist the development of a range of ser-vices designed to support families in their responsibilities in the rearing and development of children ... and to stimulate innovative thinking' (Wolcott 1989: 30). By 1980, there were slightly more than 30 services operating. In 1985, after the pilot services had operated for some years, a report to the Council of Welfare Ministers recommended that ' ... it is now appropriate for both Commonwealth and state funding authorities to commit themselves to the Family Support Program as a permanent structure in the welfare area.'

The Commonwealth withdrew from total funding of the Family Support Scheme in 1986–87 and instituted joint state and Commonwealth cost sharing of the scheme under the new title, National Family Support Program. The goal of this programme was to provide families with resources to meet the ordinary and extraordinary pressures and responsibility of family life. The National Objectives included:

- parenting support;
- service development with an emphasis on prevention and education;
- development of generic rather than specialised services;
- co-ordination and co-location of services within existing community structures in order to avoid service duplication and ensure accessibility;
- services to be available to all families, with priority being given to families identified as having greater needs.

In the three years following the establishment of the National Family Support Program, 115 Family Support Projects were funded in New South Wales. From 1989 to 1990 the funding of the programme became entirely the responsibility of the state government.

The Evolution of Family Support Services

Early family support services offered a home visiting service and centre-based group activities to families in the area it served. The community-based model provided an avenue for families to participate and so become active contributors to both their own and the community's welfare. Workers were selected on the basis of their life skills rather than professional qualifications. They were often women from the same community who were regarded as natural helpers adept at tapping resources and manoeuvring within their social network. However, funding began to come on-stream for professional training and, by 1993, 78 per cent of family workers and 93 per cent of co-ordinators had undertaken tertiary studies.

Services in New South Wales (NSW)

In 1999, the Family Support Services Association of NSW had over 130 members providing over 170 Services. Of these, the Department of Community Services (DoCS), through the Community Services Grants Program (CSGP), funded 125 organisations providing 133 family support service outlets.

Services in 1999 were working with 3,400 families in their homes at any one time and with approximately 14,000 in a full year. The population of NSW in 1998 was approximately six million and family support services worked with approximately one in 140 households. A breakdown of this population reveals that 56 per cent were lone parent families (compared with 20 per cent of the population); 78 per cent were receiving pensions or benefits; 38 per cent were in public housing (compared with 7 per cent of the population); 78 per cent were renting (compared with 30 per cent of the population); 51 per cent had children who had been notified as being at risk; and more than 43 per cent were in situations where domestic violence was an issue (Family Support Association of NSW, 1999).

A continuum of service provision from prevention to crisis intervention is provided. Universally available preventative services (primary prevention) include recreational and educational activities and services which help to build self-esteem and create social networks for service users. Early intervention services (secondary prevention) assist any family experiencing particular stress and families identified as 'at risk'. These services may include individual or family counselling and individual or group activities for families where particular concerns, such as child protection and drug and alcohol problems, have been identified. Intensive, crisis intervention services (tertiary prevention) offer assistance at times of crisis to avoid family breakdown, removal of children or to protect family members from violence. These services may include assistance for families affected by domestic violence, families with inadequate housing or other basic material needs. These are usually short-term and intensive services. Community development work, which serves to increase social capital by enhancing informal networks for families who may otherwise be socially isolated, is a feature of many services. Family support services have a 'gateway' function insofar as they operate as a gateway to other agencies and organisations that can deal with problems and difficulties which require a response or a resource which is beyond the scope or expertise of the family support service.

Onyx and Bullen's (1999) study of social capital in five New South Wales communities revealed that:

- It is possible to measure social capital in local communities.
- Within the general population, social capital is not generally related to economic well-being (i.e. more money and education does not necessarily mean more social capital). But, in more marginal circumstances, low levels of economic well-being are connected to low levels of social capital.
- The fabric of social capital in communities varies significantly from one community to another.
- Family support service users are extremely disadvantaged: they are from areas with low social capital, have minimal financial and material resources, are in stress and crisis, have relatively low levels of human capital initially but increase their levels of social capital over the time services are provided.

Figure 4.1 illustrates critical social capital connections.

The Stronger Families and Community Strategy 2000–2004

In 2000 the Australian Government launched its Stronger Families and Communities Strategy. The strategy set out a new and groundbreaking policy direction that focused on prevention, early intervention and capacity-building initiatives to help support and strengthen Australian families and communities. As part of the strategy, over 600 projects were funded across Australia. This innovative government policy focused on assisting local communities to work together in addressing factors that impact on the healthy development of Australian families and communities. With funding of AU$225 million, the strategy was underpinned by a set of eight key principles:

1. Working together in partnerships.
2. Encouraging a preventative and early intervention approach.
3. Supporting people through life transitions.
4. Developing better integrated and co-ordinated services.
5. Developing local solutions to local problems.

6. Building capacity.
7. Using the evidence and looking to the future.
8. Making the investment count.

FIGURE 4.1: SOCIAL CAPITAL CONNECTIONS

Social Capital - Social Fabric

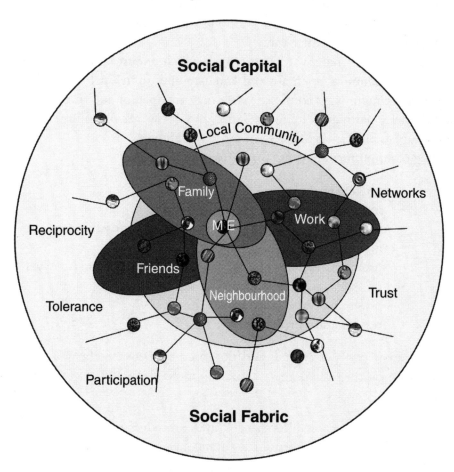

Copyright © 2000 Paul Bullen
Management Alternatives Pty Ltd Sydney (02) 9665 7737
http://www.mapl.com.au

Source: Bullen, P. and Onyx, J. (1999), *Social Capital: Family Support Services and Neighbourhood and Community Centres in New South Wales,* Sydney: Family Support Services Association of NSW.

Community Capacity Building

Community capacity building is defined as 'the combined influence of a community's commitment, resources and skills that can be deployed to build on community strengths and address community problems and opportunities' (FaCSIA 2004: 1).

Capacity building is achieved by increasing the personal and collective resources of individuals and communities, to help them develop the skills and capacities they need to respond to challenges and to seize opportunities that come their way.

Community strength – 'the extent to which resources and processes within a community maintain and enhance both individual and collective well-being in ways consistent with the principles of equity, comprehensiveness, participation, self-reliance and social responsibility'(Black and Hughes 2001) – is boosted by capacity building.
Strong communities are those that:

- provide clean, safe environments;
- meet the basic needs of residents;
- comprise residents that respect and support each other;
- involve the community in local government;
- promote and celebrate their historical and cultural heritage;
- provide easily accessible health services;
- possess a diverse, innovative economy;
- rest on a sustainable ecosystem.

Different types of capital, and the interplay between them, have a bearing on capacity building at a community level. Such types of capital include:

- human capital (levels of skills, knowledge and health status);
- social and institutional capital (leadership, motivation and networks);
- economic capital (local services, infrastructure, resources).

Table 4.1 sets out the components of community capacity.

In the Australian Government's evaluation of the Stronger Families and Community Strategy 2000–2004, several reasons are advanced for identifying the different factors that influence capacity building. More

TABLE 4.1: OVERVIEW OF COMPONENTS OF COMMUNITY CAPACITY – HUMAN CAPITAL, SOCIAL CAPITAL, INSTITUTIONAL CAPITAL AND ECONOMIC CAPITAL

Human capital: the capacity of people through their skills, knowledge and health status, to contribute to the well-being of their community:

- Skills and knowledge (including subject matter specific knowledge and skills such as problem solving).
- Capacity to adjust to changing circumstances.
- Capacity to innovate and find new solutions.
- Ability to contribute through participation, willingness to participate.
- Skills in social interaction and decision making.
- Health status – physical and mental.

Social capital: the connections amongst individuals and groups.

- Social networks and norms of reciprocity and trustworthiness that can contribute to the well-being of the community.
- Types of relationships including those that involve bonding and/or bridging capital and those that take place within family and social contexts, civic contexts, not-for-profit organisations and volunteering contexts, or involve linkages with other types of organisations and expert systems.
- Quality of relationships, including whether they are characterised by trust, altruism, reciprocity, norms, tolerance and belief in equality of opportunity, a sense of belonging in the community and self-reliance and self-help.

Institutional capital: the capacity of 'institutions' (e.g. nurturing organisations) to plan, undertake and sustain or build on activities that can contribute to the well-being of the community.

- Leadership – identification, development and exercise thereof.
- Structures and processes, including those relating to governance, culture, group work, team building, training, resolving conflict at individual, group or community levels, access to and use of networks, partners, and diverse sources of interest and expertise.
- Infrastructure, systems and facilities, including information systems.

Continued ...

Economic capital: the economic resources of the community at all levels that can be accessed to contribute to the well-being of the community.

- Economic resources associated with individuals, families and households (e.g. income, home ownership etc.).
- Economic resources associated with businesses and other organisations (e.g. investment in infrastructure).
- Public infrastructure and facilities within a community (i.e. hard infrastructure such as roads, social infrastructure such as hospitals and soft infrastructure such as medical professionals).

Source: Information compiled from FaCSIA (2004), *Evaluation of the Stronger Families and Communities Strategy 2000–2004: Community Capacity Building,* Department of Families, Community Services and Indigenous Affairs, Australia, available at: <http://www.facsia.gov.au/internet/facsinternet.nsf>.

understanding of these factors can be useful in developing an analytical framework that maps out the expectations and achievements of the strategy. By gaining a better appreciation of the potential to develop different types of capacity, communities can widen their approaches to project development and be more productive in achieving strategic outcomes.

A Capacity Building Project – The Gilles Plains Community Garden

An evaluation of the Gilles Plains Community Garden, a project that received funding under the Stronger Families and Communities Strategy, provides insights into how this capacity can be developed and utilised to help support and strengthen families and communities.

Community gardens are defined as 'places where people can come together to grow fresh food, to learn, relax and make new friends' (Australian Community Gardens Network, <http://www.communitygarden.org.au/index.html>).

In 1977, the first Australian community garden was established in Nunawading, Melbourne, in order to reduce social isolation and engage unemployed young people in a positive activity. In 1994, a Community Gardens Network linking people interested in community gardening across Australia began to promote the benefits of community gardening and facilitate the development and maintenance of gardens through information dissemination and advice. The Gilles Plain Evaluation Report (FaCSIA 2004) sets out the research evidence that supports the claim that a community garden has the potential to produce environmental, health, psychological and social benefits for individuals, families and communities.

The Gilles Plains Community Garden is located in a disadvantaged, culturally diverse suburb of Adelaide. After a gestation period lasting roughly eighteen months, garden construction commenced in 2001. The project was partly funded by the Stronger Families and Communities Strategy. While the garden is open to all members of the community, its target group includes disadvantaged families and community members in the Gilles Plains area. The management group is made up of fifteen to twenty representatives drawn from the Adelaide Central Community Health Service, the local Primary School, Child Care Centre, Aboriginal Reference Group, Anglican Church, Community House, Domestic Violence Support Group and local residents. It has been meeting since early 2000.

A basic assessment of the project 'suggests that the project effectively applied a bottom-up approach whereby professional community development workers from the local health service engaged the community who then played an active role in both developing and planning the garden as well as putting the policy into practice (i.e. constructing the garden)' (FaCSIA 2004: 21).

Unlike direct service delivery projects, where the main focus is on a short- to medium-term outcome for participants, the focus of the community garden is on direct outcomes for participants and building capacity for future activity. Table 4.2 and Table 4.3 illustrate the general outcomes and the capacity building outcomes of the Gilles Plains Community Garden project for participants, respectively.

Irish Counterparts

The family centre – the story of which is recounted in Chapter Three – developed a similar capacity-building project:

> The project began in March 2003 on a waste piece of land, which was centrally located in the estate. The aim of the project is to develop a community garden for the people of the community. The — Education Services are currently running classes in organic gardening. This garden will provide environmental education to all and will enhance community development in the area. (Fitzgerald 2004: 24)

TABLE 4.2: DIRECT OUTCOMES FOR PARTICIPANTS

Social:	• Sense of working together to accomplish something • Sense of belonging • Shared recreation with family
Economic:	• Development of skills and knowledge related to gardening and plants
Environmental:	• Improved attractiveness of physical environment • Increased awareness of water conservation, waste management, organic gardening, composting
Psychological:	• Sense of well-being and satisfaction • Calming atmosphere
Health:	• Improved mental health

TABLE 4.3: BUILDING CAPACITY FOR FUTURE ACTIVITIES

Types of Capital:	• Examples from the Gilles Plains Community Garden
Human Capital:	• Secondary and TAFE students' knowledge of history and culture of the area, biology and science of plant growth, food production and preparation • Horticulture skills development of volunteers
Economic (including Environmental) Capital:	• Physical infrastructure of the garden which allows further developments
Social Capital:	• Co-operation between individuals. • Encouraging participation in organisations
Institutional Capital:	• Development of working group membership, processes and principles • Co-operation between organisations

Source: FaCSIA (2004), *Evaluation of the Stronger Families and Communities Strategy 2000–2004: Gilles Plains Community Garden Case Study,* Department of Families, Community Services and Indigenous Affairs, Australia, available at: <http://www.facsia.gov.au/internet/facsinternet.nsf>.

Knocknaheeny/Farranree Springboard Garden

This garden is a creative endeavour which has provided an opportunity for growth and development for parents and children living in a neighbourhood of high stress in Cork City. Locals took ownership of clearing and utilising an overgrown garden, attached to the house accommodating the Springboard Project. A number of groups sprang out of this initiative. Forty children participated at the initial stage. Children have 'adopted' plants and cared for them. Because the garden has generated a positive sense of ownership, the project building has not been vandalised.

The Way Forward in Australia

Under the auspices of the Stronger Families and Communities Strategy 2004–2009, the Australian Government is seeking to achieve better outcomes for children aged up to five years and their families. The focus is on early childhood initiatives and resources that can be used to achieve better outcomes for children, their families and communities. Funding of AU$490 million has been committed for 2004–2009. There are four strands in the new strategy:

1. Communities for Children (AU$142 million over four years) is based on national and international evidence which recognises that the early years of a child's life are critical to his or her future development. Taking a community development approach to improving outcomes for young children and their families, the new initiative incorporates key principles such as collaborative action, building on community strengths and contributing to family and community capacity building.
2. Early Childhood – Invest to Grow (AU$70 million over four years) is providing funding for early childhood programmes and resources which are improving outcomes for young children through prevention and early intervention.
3. Local Answers (AU$137 million over five years) is encouraging local responsibility for self-help activities by funding small-scale, time-limited projects in disadvantaged communities. The Local Answers strand of the strategy is intended to encourage self-reliance which helps communities to build skills and capacity.

4. Choice and Flexibility in Child Care (AU$125 million over four years) is providing in-home care (IHC) packages to families with no mainstream childcare options. The following families are eligible for this service: families in remote or rural areas; families working non-standard hours; families with multiple children under school age; and families where either the parent or child has a chronic or terminal illness. A further measure in this strand will increase the supply of childcare services in areas of high unmet demand. Funding will also be used to extend the established Child Care Quality Assurance Framework into new areas.

SUPPORTING FAMILIES IN THE UK

The Children Act 1989

The purpose of the Children Act 1989 was to enshrine in law a new approach to safeguarding and promoting the welfare of children. The scope, role and overall importance of family support in progressing this new approach was set out in Part III and Schedule 2 of the Act. Under this Act, local authorities have a duty to respond to children in need by providing family centres (Schedule 2, para. 9) directly or by assisting other service providers (voluntary, private) to establish such services (section 17(5)). According to section 17(10) of the 1989 Act, a child is regarded as being in 'need' if:

1. he is unlikely to achieve or maintain, or to have the opportunity of achieving or maintaining, a reasonable standard of health or development without the provision for him of services by the local authority;
2. his health or development is likely to be significantly impaired, or further impaired, without the provision for him of such services; or
3. he is disabled.

Holistic definitions of 'development' and 'health' are spelt out in section 11 of the Act. 'Development' refers to physical, intellectual, emotional, and social and behavioural outcomes. 'Health' refers to both physical and mental well-being. The role and responsibilities of family centres are extensive under the Act. Any child, parent, carer or person with parental responsibility may avail of occupational, social, cultural or recreational activities in order to benefit from advice, guidance or counselling. Furthermore, local authorities are instructed not to restrict support services to families identified as having children at risk.

Limited progress was made in realising the family support aspirations of the Act. A bias towards child protection stymied the realignment of family services. A succession of studies and government reports (Department of Health 1995; Aldgate and Tunstill 1995; Colton *et al.* 1995) advocated a more central role for family centres in safeguarding and promoting the welfare of children and their parents. The introduction of new children's service plans created channels for new governance structures to emerge between social services and other agencies, which would harmonise the planning and provision of services for children in need. A central proposition contained in the Act was the engagement of parents in child welfare provision. Underpinning this shift towards new governance structures was the idea of partnership between parents and the social services. However, the movement towards partnership was also to include:

- Intra-local authority departmental co-operation and collaboration.
- Co-operation and collaboration between local authority social services departments and other public sector organisations.
- Co-operation and collaboration between local authority social services departments and voluntary organisations.

Many families have multiple needs and require multi-agency intervention. Such inter-agency working includes the following definitions and actions:

- Communication – one agency tells another what it intends to do.
- Consultation – one agency asks another for opinion, information or advice before finalising a plan.
- Collaboration – independent service provision with joint planning and agreement on responsibilities and boundaries.

- Bilateral planning – an overlap in service provision with operational interaction arising out of common planning.
- Joint planning – different agencies working operationally to the same plan.

Possible impediments and barriers to collaboration might include:

- Structural – fragmentation of service responsibilities across agency boundaries within and between sectors; inter-organisational complexity and lack of clarity of boundaries.
- Procedural – differences in procedures, planning horizons and cycles.
- Financial – differences in funding mechanisms and bases; and in stocks and flows of financial resources.
- Professional – differences in ideologies and values; professional self-interest and concern for threats to autonomy and domain; threats to job security; conflict of views about the interests and roles of service users.
- Status and legitimacy – organisational self-interest and concern for threats to autonomy and domain; differences in legitimacy between appointed and elected agencies. (Tunstill *et al.* 2007)

Family Support under New Labour

The coming into power of the New Labour Government in 1997, committed to tackling child poverty and social exclusion, paved the way for the introduction of new approach to family support. Influenced by Anthony Giddens' theories on the social investment state, New Labour's strategies for promoting the well-being of children and families were focused on offering welfare recipients a hand-up rather than a hand-out:

> The guideline is investment in *human capital* wherever possible, rather than the direct provision of economic maintenance. In place of the welfare state we should put the *social investment state*, operating in the context of a positive welfare society. (Giddens 1998: 117)

A three-strand policy approach, in harmony with the concept of human capital investment, was devised to deliver on these aspirations:

- Generic support for all parents with children – increasing child benefit, tax relief for children, the introduction of a national childcare strategy, and improving maternity and paternity leave.
- Designated and targeted support for poor families with children – working tax credit, the child tax credit and the childcare tax credit, welfare-to-work encouragement through personal advisors, and financial support and training.
- Programmes and initiatives targeted at disadvantaged children who are 'at risk' of being socially excluded – e.g. Sure Start, Connexions.

Programmes such as Sure Start, Connexions and On Track emerged from one of the Government's cross-cutting reviews (HM Treasury 1998), which looked at services for young children and the reasons why such services appeared, in many cases, not to be meeting their needs. The review highlighted the value of using area-based provision to promote the physical, intellectual, social and emotional development of children. Specifically, it concluded that:

> The provision of a comprehensive community-based programme of early intervention and family support which built on existing services could have positive and persistent effects and lead to significant long-term gain to the Exchequer. (Glass 1999: 261)

Sure Start programmes were rolled out in specific localities within disadvantaged areas. The guiding principles are:

1. Working with parents and children.
2. Flexible at the point of delivery.
3. Starting very early.
4. Respectful and transparent.
5. Community driven and professionally co-ordinated.
6. Outcome driven.

The programmes set out to provide:

1. Early intervention supports (activities, events, crèche facilities) for parents.

2. Improved access to health and preventive services (speech and language support).
3. Points of contact – breast-feeding café, international café, busy bees group.
4. Parent training, book-keeping, IT.
5. Pathways to employability.

A small-scale evaluation carried out by Houston (2005) found that Sure Start did create social capital by providing opportunities for networking, skill building, volunteering, support and caring. The less formal style and non-judgemental approach of the programme allowed parents 'to have a go', seek help or join. Essentially the programme was regarded as a positive supportive local structure in the community for the community.

Every Child Matters *and the Children Act 2004*

The public inquiry into the tragic death of eight-year-old Victoria Climbie produced the Laming Report in 2003. This report highlighted the unsatisfactory manner in which information was exchanged within and between agencies such as health, education, police and social services. Spurred on by the Laming Report, the Government set in motion a widespread programme of organisational reform in children's services, with the intention of progressing its ideas about early intervention and prevention. The children's green paper *Every Child Matters* (September 2003) set out the Government's commitment to improving outcomes for all children and young people – including the most disadvantaged. Five outcomes were specified in the green paper:

- being healthy;
- staying safe;
- enjoying and achieving;
- making a positive contribution;
- achieving economic well-being.

Both the green paper *Every Child Matters* (September 2003) and its follow-up document, *Every Child Matters: Next Steps* (March 2004) recognised that the realisation of this ambition entailed:

- the improvement and integration of universal services in early-years settings, schools and the health service;
- more specialised help to promote opportunity, prevent problems and act early and effectively if and when problems arise;
- the reconfiguration of services around the child and family in one place, e.g. children's centres, extended schools and the bringing together of professionals in multi-disciplinary teams;
- dedicated and enterprising leadership at all levels of the system;
- the development of a shared sense of responsibility across agencies for safeguarding children and protecting them from harm;
- listening to children, young people and their families when assessing and planning service provision, as well as in face-to-face delivery.

(Department for Education and Skills 2004: 4)

This framework for change is underpinned by the Children Act 2004 (November 2004) which constitutes the legislative spine for the implementation of the following reforms:

- a children's commissioner to champion the views and interests of children and young people;
- a duty on local authorities to set up local Safeguarding Children boards and on key partners to take part;
- provision for indexes or databases containing basic information about children and young people to enable better sharing of information;
- a requirement on local authorities to appoint a director of children's services and designate a lead member;
- the creation of an integrated inspection framework and the conduction of Joint Area reviews to assess the progress of local areas in improving outcomes; and
- provisions relating to foster care, private fostering and the education of children in care.

(Department for Education and Skills 2004: 5)

The Change for Children programme outlined in the 2004 *Every Child Matters* green paper represents an ambitious commitment to more effective co-ordination at every level, from government through commissioning of services to delivery in local communities. National responsibility for children's services has been transferred from the Department of Health to the Department of Education and Skills and, at the local level, new governance structures – children's trusts – are to provide the basis for harnessing the contribution of all agencies working with children, young people and families in the planning, commissioning and delivery of universal and targeted services. A new post of director of children's services has been established to take on the lead role in ensuring that strategic arrangements are in place to secure integrated front-line delivery across the full range of voluntary, statutory and community services.

A strengthened role for universal services within the Whole-System Change programme is intended to secure a shift from intervention to prevention. Over an eight-year period, from 2002 onwards, non-stigmatizing child and family services will be strengthened by the introduction of 3,500 children's centres, dealing with younger pre-school children, and the introduction of 'extended schools', dealing with school-age children.

CONCLUSION

In this chapter I have examined some key aspects of family and community support in Australia and the UK. In essence, the declared Australian approach has been to build community capacity in order to strengthen families and communities. As always, however, the outcome of the programmes and policies described in this chapter will depend heavily on how readily funding is made available for family support projects and the subsequent implementation processes which are set in motion. Critics such as Mowbray remain sceptical about the commitment of the Australian Government to its avowed community building policies:

> Government-dominated programmes should not be misleadingly and simplistically reported as bottom-up and 'community-driven', as breaking with traditional approaches, or as genuine partnerships (Phillips and Oxley 2002: 4). Rather than being about any substantial social transformation, community-building projects are generally about the kind of low-key and modest local activities and

services that people pursue despite government. Not matched by the reality, the grandiose claims about community building need to be understood substantively as instances of ideological opportunism. (2005: 263)

In the UK the Children Act 1989 attempted to expand the role of family support services in safeguarding and protecting children. The resources required to implement the more extended family support provisions of the Act were not forthcoming. Investigation of 'at risk' situations claimed the lion's share of resources and as a result a re-balancing of child welfare services did not occur.

The social inclusion agenda of the New Labour Government of 1997 has led to a massive investment in services for children. Extensive organisational and strategic changes have been set in train by the Green Paper proposals and the new Children Act 2004. These ambitious reforms stem from New Labour's active citizenship approach to social integration and social cohesion. As such, they are directed towards the formation of human and social capital amongst marginalised sections of the population who pose a threat to social cohesion and the total social enterprise. This chapter and Chapter Three have provided narrative accounts of the origins, policy frameworks and service delivery approaches of some family support services operating in Ireland, the UK and Australia. The next chapter focuses on the practice models applied to these systems.

CHAPTER FIVE

PRACTICE STORIES

INTRODUCTION

As we have seen, effective family support is inextricably linked with community development and the creation of social capital. The relationship between community development and family support in the Irish context is explored more deeply in this chapter. Links between family support, community development and social capital formation are then explored in the context of two contemporary Irish community development initiatives. The impact of these links on the practice of social workers and social care workers engaging in community-based family support work is outlined. Drawing on examples of best practice in the US, Australia and the UK, the final section of the chapter proposes a new model of service delivery for family support. Areas addressed in this chapter include:

- Background to community development and family support in Ireland over the past thirty years.
- Family Support in the Health Service Executive (HSE).
- The Springboard programme.
- The connection between family support, community development and social capital, the practice of which is seen in the Government's RAPID programme (launched in 2000) and the ongoing civic renewal in the Dublin docklands area.
- Examples of best practice in the US, Australia and the UK are analysed and a new model for community-oriented family support practice is put forward.

COMMUNITY DEVELOPMENT

According to Hodge (1970):

> The literature on community development is extensive yet frequently verbose and turgid, and rarely trenchant. Practitioners and exponents tend to be zealots and purists, particularly with their own interpretation of community development. The more successful are indeed rare and gifted persons, singular in dedication. Their common fault is an inability to explain what they do and what are their skills. (1970: 66)

The roots of community development as a professional activity are to be found in the historical traditions of:

- *Informal self-help and solidarity,* characterised by reciprocity and sharing behaviours within the small-scale structures of social organisation. Relationships forged from feelings shared and interests held in common are manifested in neighbourliness.
- *Mutual aid,* whereby formal structures were put in place to supply help and shared resources to a given membership.
- *Philanthropy and voluntary service* directed towards the needy.

Informed by these three strands, community development became associated with *remedial, preventative* and *governance strategies.*

Remedial strategies were intended to counteract the factors preventing residents in poor communities from overcoming their disadvantages and utilising opportunities for personal advancement and democratic engagement. An example of this approach was the work of the University Settlements, whereby university students on temporary placements combined adult education with 'character-building' activities.

Preventative strategies sought to organise and foster autonomous voluntary groups which could create a buffer zone between the impersonal institutions of the state and the individual. Workers were frequently employed by state welfare agencies.

Governance strategies became synonymous with the British colonial system. Community development as an export model was conjured up in the 1920s by colonial officials and educationists to compensate for the inadequacies of the conventional school system in the colonies. As such, it was seen as a vehicle for the transition from colonial status to self rule in the context of economic and social change. Initially, formal education in school had been considered as the key to general progress. However experience taught that, to attain the advancement of the whole community, there was needed, in addition to an improved system of schools, advancement in other nation-building programmes for health, industry, agriculture and civic education.

Within this early model of community development the focus was on specific localities, and effort was concentrated on maximising the benefits of the positive aspects of community life – solidarity, mutualism and processes of co-operation. Operationally, community was regarded as an area of social functioning marked by levels of social coherence. Pivotal aspects of community were locality and community sentiment.

By the 1970s, a new profession had emerged in the UK which combined two related approaches:

> The first saw the community as a resource, a partner, in the provision of welfare services. Problems could be addressed by involving local residents in developing collective solutions. As well as supplying volunteer staff, community associations and other locally based voluntary organisations were seen as potential managers of projects supplying social care for older people, health education, benefits advice and childcare (Reinold 1974; Clarke 1990). The second approach was similar, but placed more emphasis on personal fulfilment, regarding community involvement as a vehicle for self-improvement. Taking part in community activities was seen as therapeutic (staving off mental health problems), morally worthy (encouraging mutuality and social responsibility) and educational (promoting the acquisition of skills and new understandings). Adult education classes and cultural societies were seen as 'improving' in themselves, while recreational activities such as youth clubs and sport associations were encouraged as a means of diverting people from a life of crime, idleness and social isolation. (Gilchrist 2004: 14–15)

Integrating Community Development and Family Support

The great divide in community development work is broadly between consensus and conflict approaches to practice. Community action, a form of practice which gained currency in the UK (Gilchrist 2004) and the US (Holman 1978) in the 1970s and 1980s, attempted to use conflict to achieve change. Practitioners campaigned against the status quo and sought to verbalise discontent, articulate grievances, build alliances with the labour movement and form pressure groups in a militant struggle for social justice. Within the consensus tradition the emphasis is on gradualist practice strategies. Characterised by a non-directive approach, the practitioner has an enabling or facilitating role in self-help projects, self-sustaining local improvement and devising responses to felt needs. In order to provide a brief account of the traditions of a complex enterprise such as community development, differences in practice orientation have been simplified. For Twelvetrees (1991), a distinction can be made between radical and professional community work. Professional community workers are paid and have specialist skills. They have an enabling role with community groups and assist them in running self-help or campaigning activities. It is also part of their brief to try and ensure that statutory and other service providers deliver services more effectively so that they meet community needs better. Radical community work confronts social and economic arrangements which systematically oppress certain groups, for instance people living in absolute or relative poverty, women, and ethnic and racial minorities. Because radical community workers are attempting to create radical change in society, they do not accept that they should be bound, in their work, by rules which stem from oppressive hierarchical structures:

> Community workers from this 'radical' tradition, which has its roots in the politics of dissent, have tended to search for 'oppositional' ways of working which challenge the status quo. In the early 1970s this often took the form of organising militant campaigns, seeking to build links with organisations such as trade unions, making propaganda, and seeking to get alternative issues on public agendas. (Twelvetrees 1991: 5)

COMMUNITY DEVELOPMENT AND FAMILY SUPPORT IN IRELAND

Community action or radical community work failed to make an impact in Ireland. As Gilligan (1991) has suggested, community workers were employed in Ireland by statutory bodies to lubricate relations between bureaucratic state agencies and local communities. The main employers of community workers in Ireland circa 1990 were health boards or local voluntary bodies. While health boards were allowed considerable flexibility in deploying community workers, their functions as a rule included the following:

- To assess needs.
- To develop awareness of needs.
- To advise on priorities.
- To promote, maintain and develop the potential of voluntary groups who were promoting or providing social service.
- To develop and maintain liaison between these groups and relevant statutory agencies.
  (NESC 1987: 50)

Community workers were given responsibility, under section 65 of the 1953 Health Act, for grant aiding voluntary and community organisations providing services 'similar or ancillary' to those provided by health boards.

The appointment of community workers was unevenly spread across the then eight Health Boards. Some boards (South-Eastern, Midlands, North-Eastern) never appointed community workers. In other boards (Mid-Western, Eastern) community work posts were converted to social work posts.

The Southern Health Board had a longstanding investment in community work. Table 5.1 sets out the development of community work in the Southern Health Board.

The Task Force Report on Child Care Services, 1980

In the UK and the US community work was conceived of as being the third method of social work, i.e. complementary to casework with individuals or families and group work (Henderson and Thomas 2002).

TABLE 5.1: SOUTHERN HEALTH BOARD COMMUNITY WORK DEVELOPMENT

1974
Five posts created in the Southern Health Board area 'to help voluntary groups with the organisation and development of services for the aged'.

1979
Seven community work posts established to include work in relation to pre-schools, youth services, family support services, specific interest groups and work with the elderly.

1985
Community work becomes a distinct and separate discipline within the Community Care programme.

1995
Creation of regional (Southern Health Board wide) senior community work post.

2000–2001
Four additional principal community work posts (one per Community Care Area) plus nineteen basic grade posts established.

In Ireland, the final report of the Task Force on Child Care Services (September 1980) recommended that community development and community youth work be included in family support services. The Task Force report envisaged a considerable increase in social workers, childcare workers and youth and community workers to implement its proposals. While the main report recommended the establishment of a statutory Child Care Authority with responsibility for the childcare system at regional level and that the existing health boards should carry out the functions to be assigned to the Child Care Authority, a supplementary section of the report queried the designation of health boards as Child Care Authorities. The supplementary section recommended that the Child Care Authorities should oversee the establishment of a new family and child care programme to facilitate the integration of childcare and family support services.

It was suggested that the existing community care programmes within the health boards, with their emphasis on medical care, could not deliver community services and family support services – the essential foundations of the work of the Child Care Authority:

Almost all the services recommended by the Task Force will be linked to, or dependent on, family support and community services. The only exceptions will be family placement services for children who need permanent family placement, adoption or sometimes long-term foster care. Therefore, practically all the functions of the Child Care Authority would be considered either to derive from the family support and community services functions or to be dependent on those services for their success. (Task Force on Childcare Services 1980: 385)

Neighbourhood resource centres (which were also recommended by the main report) were to be the focus of the Child Care Authorities' family's support and community services. The services to be provided, supported and co-ordinated in any given community included:

- home help services;
- special childcare services and social work services for children and their families in their own homes;
- day care services (playgroups, day nurseries and crèches, out-of-school care, child-minding services);
- community work;
- community youth work services;
- social work services in association with schools.

Both the main report and the supplementary section stressed the need for integration of all childcare and family support services and liaison with other essential services such as health, education, housing and environmental amenities, and income maintenance.

In Henderson's view, community work is one of a number of possible methods or approaches that can support community development and community work with children and families (in Henderson and Thomas 2002). He distinguishes between community work carried out with and on behalf of children in cooperation with parents and other adults, and community work which is targeted more directly at young people and which may overlap with youth work. Henderson's analysis, almost twenty years after the final report of the Task Force (1980), is in broad agreement with that report's recommendations 22, 23, 24 and 25 on the central importance of 'community' for the welfare of children.

Alongside the home and school it is where children learn and develop. This, fundamentally, is why community work with children is of critical significance. Community is, alongside family and educational facilities, a Child Development System. It is where children establish associations, gain identity and develop social skills through play, investigation and interaction with peer groups. (Callaghan and Dennis in Henderson and Thomas 2002: 6)

Community work was to have played a pivotal part in the new family and childcare programme advocated by the Task Force on Child Care Services in its final report (1980). The Task Force report highlighted the need for the integration of childcare and family support services within a new programme. Such a programme was never established and 'the dominant focus in childcare services since the early 1990s has been on the protection and care of children who are at risk' (Dolan *et al.* 2006: 13).

So, in both practical and conceptual terms, Irish personal social services have been organised around the tasks and protocols of 'safeguarding' children and 'correcting' individual malfunctions (O'Doherty 2004). Interventions by welfare professionals such as social workers are intended to remedy a wide range of social problems. The role of the social worker, in this organisational context, is to identify, assess and intervene in problem situations located at the level of individuals or family systems and to rectify identified shortcomings. The purpose of the intervention is not to transform living conditions or institutional structures involving 'fundamental adjustments of the social environments' (Hardiker *et al.* 1991), but to maintain order and social functioning.

Child Care Act 1991

During the 1990s, a major debate opened up in the UK about the future direction of social work policy and practice. The debate crystalised around the 1989 Children Act which sought to integrate policies and practices in child protection with support for 'children in need':

The Children Act 1989 introduced the concept of children in need as a central theme, underlining the importance of family support services which may be provided to the child, the family, or any individual, provided that this is aimed at safe guarding or promoting the child's welfare. (Association of Directors of Social Services/National Children Homes 1996: 3)

While academics, government policy makers and practitioners in the UK were engaging in a major 'refocusing debate' (refocusing child protection in the context of children in need) throughout the 1990s, the Irish statutory service providers (health boards – now the Health Service Executive (HSE)) failed to capitalise on the opportunities provided by the 1991 Child Care Act for engaging in a similar re-focusing debate.

In Ireland one of the most fundamental changes in the legal framework for child and family social work services has been the implementation of the Child Care Act 1991. As the first piece of modern legislation in Ireland to deal with children in a comprehensive manner, it sets out a continuum of service interventions which the Health Service Executive is required to provide. The continuum model makes it possible for HSE social workers to treat services as complementary rather than compartmentalised or even in opposition. Rather than making an issue of the relative merits of family support versus protection, the continuum model endorses the involvement of social workers in the particular challenge of intervening in the complex set of interacting factors at individual, family and community levels, thus influencing the development of children and young people and their subsequent life chances in adulthood. The HSE is obliged under section 3 of the 1991 Child Care Act to provide family support services to promote the welfare of children not receiving adequate care and attention. At the beginning of the nineties, the passing and subsequent implementation of the Child Care Act indicated that a critical phase in the social construction of a comprehensive childcare and family support system had been reached. By 1995, Gilligan was problematising the state's commitment to activating family support policy: 'Will family support become the disowned orphan or the favoured child in terms of public policy in childcare?' (1995: 77).

In Gilligan's view, family support, jockeying for position with child protection and alternative care, ranked third in the overall field of child protection and welfare. By 1996, Murphy was observing that the concept of prevention in childcare discourse, virtually absent in the 1980s, had re-emerged in the 1990s. However, the family support model enshrined in the 1991 Act, according to Murphy (1996), advances a narrow concept of prevention, which fails to take full account of the changed life contexts of adults and children in Ireland. Key inquiry reports on the Kilkenny Incest Case (1993), Madonna House (1996) and the Kelly Fitzgerald case

(1996), highlighted the need for family support services and the development of prevention programmes. The Commission on the Family's report, *Strengthening Families for Life*, states that the development of such supportive and preventative schemes would act 'as an intrinsic and integrated approach to the problem of child abuse' (1998: 30).

The same report suggests that, while the Act does not specify the details of what is required under the provision of family support, its primary focus should be on promoting the welfare of children in vulnerable families in order to minimise those circumstances in which a child might have to be removed from her or his family and placed in alternative care. Sporadic attempts to generate a re-focusing debate, similar to the one taking place in the UK, were doomed to failure because responsibility for family support programmes had already been taken from the Department of Health and the Health Boards and given to anther government department (see next section).

Family Resource Centres and the Community Development Programme

Family resource centres, the broad infrastructure originating in the 1970s, were established by the Catholic Church and provided family support targeting disadvantaged families in an effort to break the 'cycle of disadvantage' in newly developed working-class parishes in Dublin. They provided focused, but flexible, programmes which aimed to enhance the self-esteem and potential of individuals and thereby increase the capacity of local communities to become self-reliant and self-directed.

Community Development programmes were established in 1990 by the Department of Social Welfare in recognition of the role of community development in responding to poverty and disadvantage. They provide financial assistance to specialised centres supporting women's groups, the travelling community, people out of home and people with disabilities. The Community Development programme primarily funds projects concerned with changing structures and influencing policy.

According to the Family Resource Centres report (Kelleher and Kelleher 1997), while family resource centre projects differ from projects funded under the Community Development programme, both models are important in combating poverty and can be combined within one project or parallel each other in two separate projects. The report recommended that the Department of Welfare (now Social, Community and Family Affairs), rather than the Department of Health and the health boards, be the designated lead government department for developing and mainstreaming the Family Resource Centre programme. The authors (Kelleher and Kelleher) concluded that:

1. Community development is inadequately resourced (insufficient personnel employed) in health boards and lacks a dedicated management structure. This non-allocation of resources to community development has resulted in an absence of a community development approach being understood and adopted by health boards.

2. The main priority of health boards has been child protection and the social work service is equated, in many peoples' perceptions, with child protection, notwithstanding the wide range of services, which are aimed at prevention and preventing young people falling into the 'at risk' category and needing residential care. The report acknowledges that health boards are providing services such as the Community Mothers programmes, Family Resource projects and Neighbourhood Youth projects to parents and children.

3. Health boards' funding arrangements with the voluntary sector are problematic. Such funding is routed through the Community Care programme or Section 65 of the 1970 Health Act (whereby community organisations providing services similar or ancillary to those provided by health boards can be grant aided). The demands made by health boards on projects funded directly can be at variance with the principles underlying projects directed and controlled by local people. These demands can include: limited access to services which can be restricted to referrals from health board personnel, third-level qualifications for the required staff, and the project being directly managed by the health board.

4. Health board Family Resource projects are based on a model of intervention, which is not centrally concerned with local empowerment, local control, participatory management and open access.

For these reasons, this report did not recommend that the Department of Health and the health boards be given the responsibility for developing and mainstreaming the projects, which are now the responsibility of the Department of Community, Rural and Gaeltacht Affairs. The Department of Health and Children and the ten regional health boards (now HSE) are operating under the auspices of a separate policy framework. The consequences of these decisions are that family support is integrated with community development but completely separate from health and personal social services.

In Cannan and Warren's (1997) estimation: 'children's and family services in the UK need recasting in a community development framework.' In Ireland there is also a clear need to re-embed social care and social work practice in a community development and family support framework. In one of the few Irish studies assessing the community development–family support relationship, McGrath (2003) called for a 'strategic engagement' between the HSE and community development and family support services.

Family Support in the Ten Regional Health Boards

A research study was carried out by the author between 1999 and 2003 exploring the ways in which the ten health boards (now the Health Service Executive) operationalised the general duty of each and every one of them to:

1. 'Promote the welfare of children … who are not receiving adequate care and protection.' Child Care Act 1991, 3(1)
2. 'Provide child care and family support services.' Child Care Act 1991, 3(3)

A critical objective of this research study was to map out the national contours of statutory family support policy and practice in the regional health boards. Despite a modest response rate, results suggested that narrowing the scope of social work activity in the health boards was precluding social workers from engaging in community-level practice directed at preventing child abuse and neglect. The survey data indicated that the following pressure points were contributing to this circumscription of social work activity in the health boards:

- Resource and staffing limitations.
- The prioritising of child protection over other social work activities.
- Social workers constructing a new 'hybrid identity' (Derber 1983) which entitled them to a quasi-managerial status within health boards. This quasi-managerial status was grounded in a case management style of practice that was in harmony with the wider business model then being adopted by health boards.

The survey data suggested that social workers, while protesting about the priority given to child protection work in the health boards, may themselves have been complicit in the construction and delivery of what counted as performance in social work practice in the health boards. This begs the question as to the reasons why family support work did not count as performance. Perhaps it was because it is more difficult to regulate such activity. Frost's study (1987) makes the case for development of specialist family support teams within the statutory social services (as opposed to family support being contracted out to the voluntary sector). Frost outlines the potential advantages and disadvantages of such a service.

Advantages

- The family support function remains within the social services department and thereby commits the state agency to delivering family support provision as part of its operational remit. This allows departmental staff to gain expertise and share their practice experiences and knowledge with their colleagues through training and co-working. In this way the status and profile of family support work within the statutory services sector is enhanced and assured – it has a strategic location within the organisation and will not be contracted out for others to provide.
- Since family support work takes place alongside the child protection function of the Department, communication between those working in family support and colleagues engaged in child protection work is encouraged and organisational barriers to communication are minimised.

Disadvantages

Using dedicated family support teams can send out a message that the practice of family support is a specialist one, best left to the 'experts' and therefore not of direct concern to the mainstream area teams. This approach effectively means that responsibility for family support work is not shared equally by all the area social workers. Family support work is undertaken by one specialist group of social workers while statutory child protection work remains the primary responsibility of a different group of social workers. In this way, family support becomes an adjunct to the mainstream work of the Department. Frost sets out a number of potential models that can be adopted by social services departments in relation to voluntary organisations and to the emphasis they wish to place on family support. Frost (1997) has identified a number of strategic options available to statutory social service providers, such as the HSE, in organising and structuring the delivery of child protection and family support services. Table 5.2 sets out these strategic options as a series of potential models that statutory service providers can adopt in relation to voluntary service providers and in relation to the emphasis they wish to put on family support.

The Springboard Programme

Springboard is a community based programme which aims to support vulnerable families in the home, school and community. Springboard projects are located in high stress neighbourhoods where there is a marked incidence of factors contributing to the reception of children into care. Each Springboard project has its own history and developmental pathway.

Fourteen Springboard family support projects, launched by the Government in 1998, provided instances of these operational arrangements in Ireland. The expectation of the Department of Health and Children in overseeing the development of Springboard was that the projects would achieve the following:

- Identify the needs of parents and children in a specific area, paying particular attention to families where

TABLE 5.2: FROST'S PARTNERSHIP ARRANGEMENTS

+ = High level of engagement
– = Low level of engagement

A
   Family support +
   Voluntary sector +

B
   Family support –
   Voluntary sector +

C
   Family support +
   Voluntary sector –

D
   Family support –
   Voluntary sector –

Box A – High level of engagement with the delivery of family support and the voluntary sector. Possibly realised through community based social work teams, a high level of day care and a commitment to partnership working.

Box B – Low commitment to family support, coupled with a high commitment to the voluntary sector. Statutory social work services generally focus on child protection and a defined group of children and young people in need. Other family support services are being contracted out to voluntary organisations.

Box C – A low commitment to the voluntary sector and a high commitment to family support. Statutory social work/services demonstrate this high commitment by directly providing a comprehensive family support programme incorporating community based work, day care and early supportive interventions in partnership with families. As a result, the voluntary sector has a low involvement in family support work.

Box D – Demonstrates low commitment to both family support and partnership with contracting out of such work to voluntary organisations.

Source: Frost, N. (1997), 'Delivering Family Support: Issues and Themes in Service Development' in Nigel Parton (ed.) (1997), *Child Protection and Family Support,* London: Routledge, Figure 11.1, 198.

- child protection concerns exist;
- families experience health or welfare problems;
- families are in a 'once-off' crisis situation.

• Target the most disadvantaged and vulnerable families in an area and focus on improving their parenting skills and child-parent relationships.

- Develop programmes of family support services in partnership with different agencies in an area, key groups, individuals in the community and families.
- Provide direct services through a structured package of care, intervention, support and counselling to targeted families and children, and to families within the wider community.

Seven of the Springboard projects are managed by Barnardos, two by a health board, two by a partnership between a health board and a voluntary organisation and three by a voluntary organisation. Fourteen Springboard Projects were evaluated by McKeown *et al.* in the Department of Health and Children publication, *Springboard – Promoting Family Wellbeing through Family Support Services* (2001). Their evaluation strategy involved measuring the impact of the programmes on children and parents and measuring perceptions of Springboard as a service. Professional perceptions of Springboard (based on 172 questionnaires completed by a wide range of professionals – including project staff – who are in regular contact with the Springboard project in their area) were overwhelmingly positive. For health boards:

> Springboard has been successful in halving the number of children at moderate-to-high risk of being abused or going into care.... . In this sense, therefore, the strategy of addressing child protection concerns through the family support approach of Springboard is working well and points the way towards more effective and holistic forms of intervention with vulnerable families (McKeown *et al.* 2001: 119).

The 172 professionals involved directly or indirectly with Springboard believe that it represents value for money for the following three reasons:

1. It is a cheaper option than care and/or other forms of crisis intervention.
2. It is cheaper than doing nothing and letting problems escalate.
3. It reduces pressure on child protection services which may result in some financial savings for health boards.
(McKeown *et al.* 2001: 119)

Since 2001, thirteen new Springboard projects have been established. There are now twenty-two projects operating across the country and another five have been commissioned (see Appendix A for full details). Table 5.3 sets out the range of governance structures being used in the Springboard programme.

TABLE 5.3: GOVERNANCE STRUCTURES USED IN THE SPRINGBOARD PROGRAMME

Barnardos	HSE	Kildare Youth Services	Limited Company	Foroige	Daughters of Charity
9	7	1	3	1	1

Within Frost's model of partnership arrangements, Springboard projects which come under the auspices of the HSE fall into strategic option Box B. Under such arrangements, tension may arise between state social workers and family support stakeholders operating in the voluntary sector.

Jordan's case study (1997) of one UK local authority's attempt to develop partnership between its professional service providers and the parents of children in need, explored some of the more deep-seated reasoning influencing a statutory service provider's choice of strategic option:

> As the partnership approach developed, it seemed to polarise attitudes within the social services department. At the grassroots level, while some social workers were actively engaged with groups, there was, if anything, a tendency towards a sharper distinction between child protection work and family support, with many professional staff distancing themselves from the groups, who in turn sought greater independence and separation from the child protection core of the department's work. (Jordan 1997: 213)

Attempts to move the social services department in the direction of partnership and family support activity challenged assumptions about power, responsibility, ownership and the nature of the services themselves. According to this analysis, many social workers are at best ambivalent and at worst highly resistant about abandoning a style of work which is power-laden, formal and individualised in favour of an approach which involves greater sharing in groups and more negotiated, informal work. Within the present structures of social services departments, not only is child protection work privileged but a particular kind of relationship to the department's authority structure is rewarded. Jordan argues that this 'particular type of relationship' is not conducive to a genuine partnership approach. Social workers have a stake in professionally referred and led models of family support for children in need and are reluctant to embrace the open access, neighbourhood participation approach advocated by Holman (1978), Cannan and Warren (1997) and Pithouse *et al.* (1998). In the Irish welfare system, social care workers have begun to fill the professional void created by the apparent reluctance of social workers to engage in the kind of practice which fosters social integration and a sense of community.

MAKING CONNECTIONS BETWEEN FAMILY SUPPORT, COMMUNITY DEVELOPMENT AND SOCIAL CAPITAL

Family support provision can contribute to broader community development and at the same time augment social capital levels when there is a clear understanding that family support workers, community development workers, and social work and care professionals share a common goal.

> Across a broad range of efforts, an emphasis on community building has focused fundamentally on the goal of strengthening the capacity of communities to identify priorities and opportunities, effectively support and provide for the individuals and families who live there, and work to foster and sustain positive community change. (Chaskin 2006: 43)

Chaskin (2006) presents us with an integrated model of family support as community based practice. Firstly, he charts the failure of categorical approaches to welfare services. A categorical approach to policies (Briar-Lawson *et al.* 2001) and practices exists when families are viewed separately and in isolation from other needs and priorities. Policy makers' attention is focused on categories of individuals, e.g. children or women or older people. Families are seen as just one of many sectors or categories in society competing for services. Inevitably, this leads to a proliferation of selective provision which does not take into account the relational aspects of welfare. A relational approach to family policies and practices is based on an understanding of the responsibilities, meaning and significance of families and their contribution to the societal culture. The interrelationships between families, other social institutions (e.g. schools) and other policy categories (e.g. economic) are prioritised. Relational programmes are universalistic in character, are aimed at the community as a whole, are seen as benefiting everybody and thus avoid being regarded as poor services for poor people. Table 5.4 sets out the pivotal values, commitments and practice strategies for family support work aimed at the whole community.

While acknowledging that family support services are operating in the social arena or context of community, Gilchrist's model also recognises family support as a vehicle for promoting community change. As Chaskin puts it:

> Family support programs have for the most part engaged in community largely as a critical context to understand and inform their strategic orientation to working with families, rather than as a target or medium of change. Increasingly, though, proponents of family support have sought to move beyond a community-as-context framework to argue for family support's role in promoting community change more broadly. (2006: 50)

In practice, this requires a networking approach to family support which incorporates reflective practice and a community capacity building agenda. In the following two case studies, community capacity building is facilitated by giving residents and service users more scope to control their social environment, choose their activities and set the terms of engagement with professionals.

The RAPID Programme – A Reflective Practice Approach to Capacity Building and Networking

Reflective practice is a creative process of constructing solutions, rather than a passive process of following procedures or guidelines. Social workers and social care workers engaging in community based family support work are effectively guests in the community, guests who must enter into a process of negotiation with community members around the

TABLE 5.4: VALUES, COMMITMENTS AND PRACTICE STRATEGIES USED IN FAMILY SUPPORT WORK

Values

- Social Justice – enabling people to claim their human rights, meet their needs and have greater control over the decision-making processes that affect their lives.
- Participation – facilitating democratic involvement by people in the issues that affect their lives based on full citizenship, autonomy and shared power, skills, knowledge and experience.
- Equality – challenging the attitudes of individuals and the practices of institutions and a society that discriminates against and marginalises people.
- Learning – recognising the skills, knowledge and expertise that people contribute and develop by taking action to tackle social, economic, political and environmental problems.
- Co-operation – working together to identify and implement action based on mutual respect of diverse cultures and contributions.

Commitments

- Challenging discrimination and oppressive practices within organisations, institutions and communities.
- Developing policy and practice that protects the environment.
- Encouraging networking and connections between communities and organisations.
- Ensuring access and choice for all groups and individuals within society.
- Influencing policy and programmes from the perspective of communities.
- Prioritising the issues of concern to people experiencing poverty and social exclusion.
- Promoting social change that is long-term and sustainable.
- Reversing inequality and the imbalance of power relationships in society.
- Supporting community-led collective action.

Practice Strategies

- Enabling people to become involved by removing practical barriers to their participation.
- Encouraging individuals to contribute to activities and decision making, and to keep going when things get difficult.
- Empowering others by increasing their confidence and ability to influence decisions and take responsibility for their own actions.

Continued ...

- Educating people by helping them to reflect on their own experience, to learn from others and through discussion.
- Equalising situations so that people have the same access to opportunities, resources and facilities within communities and mainstream services.
- Evaluating the impact of these interventions.
- Engaging with groups and organisations to increase community involvement in partnerships and other forms of public decision making.

Source: Gilchrist, A. (2004), *The Well-Connected Community: A Networking Approach to Community Development,* Bristol: The Policy Press.

provision of useful responses to families' needs. In endeavouring to avoid standardised, formulaic responses to the complex and dynamic needs of different families in a community or neighbourhood, helping professionals need therefore to see themselves as sources of ideas and creative solutions.

Reflective practice is increasingly seen as a way forward for nurses, family support workers, social workers, youth workers and social care workers. It encourages helping professionals not to be in thrall to theory but to engage with theory creatively and in constructive and positive ways. Using the RAPID programme as a case study in capacity building and networking practice, this section sets out the range of core skills required by programme co-ordinators who have an interest in reflective practice.

RAPID (Revitalising Areas by Planning, Investment and Development) is a focused government initiative instituted to target the 45 most disadvantaged urban areas and provincial towns in Ireland. Strand 1 was launched in 25 urban areas in February 2000 and Strand 2 was extended to twenty provincial towns in February 2002. Its aims are to:

- increase the investment made by government departments and state agencies in the 45 communities;
- improve the delivery of public services through integration and co-ordination;
- enhance the opportunities for communities to participate in the strategic improvement of their areas.

RAPID is implemented locally by a cross-sectoral Area Implementation Team and is supported by a RAPID co-ordinator. The City or County

nt Board manages the programme locally. The RAPID Na-
ιitoring Committee is chaired by the Minister for Community,
ι Gaeltacht Affairs. The RAPID programme is about building
particip∪ιtion structures within the communities of the designated areas
so that residents can make appropriate recommendations to meet their
needs. The process of building participation structures involves community members meeting, bridging, bonding and linking with professionals,
agencies, and other community leaders and members from other areas.
RAPID co-ordinators hold pivotal positions and play key roles in setting
up and servicing area-based multi-agency forums. These network-type
organisations are vehicles for the involvement of residents in decision
making structures in their own areas. RAPID co-ordinators require:

- research and information gathering skills;
- communication skills;
- group work skills;
- skills in developing strategies and tactics;
- meeting skills;
- resource management skills;
- skills in developing training and education pathways;
- people management skills.

Co-ordinators participating in capacity building networks – with
their informal mechanisms of accountability – enjoy a degree of autonomy in their work. If they are to profit from this professional autonomy,
they must monitor and reflect on their own performance and credibility.
Managers can assist practitioners to clarify their roles and to review on
a regular basis the effectiveness of their networking by asking people to
examine:

- how their relationships with people in the community are
developing and being maintained;
- the extent to which they are helping to secure resources and
facilitating processes within a community, which maintain
and enhance both individual and collective well-being in
ways consistent with the principles of equity, participation,
self-reliance and social responsibility.

Reflective practice should not be left to the frontline practitioners engaged in capacity building and networking. Managers and supervisors of such systems must also be accountable for their actions. They must seek to come to terms with the complexity, variability and uncertainty of informal networking by using experience, knowledge and theoretical perspectives to guide and inform their actions.

The Dockland Story – Regenerating Social Capital

After years of neglect and stagnation, a master plan for the regeneration of the Dublin docklands area was prepared by the Dublin Docklands Development Authority (DDDA) (established by the 1997 Act) and published in 2003. The rich cultural heritage and social cohesion of the vibrant communities in the area was acknowledged in the master plan and the needs of the five resident communities were taken into account in its strategic objectives.

Urban regeneration requires not only the physical renewal of inner cities and decaying areas, but also involves significant social, economic and environmental dimensions. This policy is reflected in the 1997 Act. The inclusive approach set out in the Act provides for a more democratic process, inviting communities to participate in and contribute to the development of their areas. This provides a broader spectrum incorporating physical, economic and social considerations, including education, training and employment opportunities (DDDA 2003).

At the fourth Dublin Docklands' Social Regeneration Conference the key assets for civic renewal were identified as:

- the capacities, gifts and skills of the residents;
- a residents' association;
- groups in the neighbourhood such as businesses, not-for-profit agencies and government;
- the place;
- the exchanges taking place – buying and selling.

These assets exist in the Docklands but require connecting to create a community which can than benefit from social capital. The connecting may be carried out by professionals and residents.

What Enables Family Support and Community Development Workers to become Strategic Networkers?

To be efficient and effective at providing services and creating social capital, family support and community development practitioners need to be:

- committed to the role of positive change agent for families and children through networking: 'The development of "community" is about strengthening and extending networks of relationships between individuals, between organisations and, just as importantly, between different sectors and agencies'(Gilchrist 2004: 25);
- guided by the values, commitments and practice strategies set out in Table 5.4 (above);
- engaged in a continuing process of reflecting on how well suited their practice approach is to their task in hand.

A NEW MODEL FOR COMMUNITY-ORIENTED FAMILY SUPPORT PRACTICE

New approaches to family support work are developing all the time and it is important to build new innovative and effective models of practice which bring together examples of best practice from different countries. This section sets out the contribution that US, Australian and UK family support strategies can make to an international model of best practice. The new synthesised model is presented in the following section.

The US Contribution to a New Model – The Massachusetts Patch Approach

The Massachusetts Patch program, currently operating in the USA, is based on the principles of community social work. The starting point of this approach can be traced back to the federal Family Preservation and Support Services Program (1993) which later fell under the auspices of the Adoption and Safe Families Act (1997). The 'Patch' strategy is to link the protection work of public child welfare with the prevention work of family support in a neighbourhood setting. This two-pronged approach focuses on:

- creating change in communities by renegotiating relationships between public child welfare agencies and the people they serve; and
- improving practice to keep children safe by strengthening the everyday capacities of families and neighbourhoods to care for their children.
(US Department of Health and Human Services Children's Bureau, 2000: 3)

Neighbourhood based teams (these teams are assigned a geographically defined caseload and they work from offices located in the communities they serve) are made up of public service social workers, their supervisors, other state agency representatives such as youth workers, community based family support agencies, a Patch team co-ordinator and others. However, there is no set definition for the make-up of the team, as the skills mix will vary according to the needs of the neighbourhood and the opportunities available for positive engagement with families. In order to bring about change in the relationships between individuals and communities which are perpetuating problems, the nature of the relationships between a whole range of significant people need to be understood and changed. According to the US Department of Health and Human Services Children's Bureau, the core skill of team leaders is 'change mapping':

Change mapping is rooted in working with a family to identify and define the social networks within which their daily lives take place. It is in this network, this fabric of relationships, that problems crop up and resources for their solutions can be found. 'Patch change mapping' draws on the tradition of solution-focused techniques, as well as familiar family-centred techniques such as the genogram and the ecomap. However, rather than having a diagnostic slant, change mapping emphasises attention to often-unrecognized resources in a family's network, resources that have the potential to encourage, facilitate and sustain the changes needed to help a family meet its goals. (2000: 13–14)

Family workers on the 'Patch' team:

- engage in direct work with families to gain understanding of the patterns that maintain problems;
- link families with tangible supports or specialised services;
- deal with unintended system effects;
- build community resources;
- advocate, within their own agencies, changes in official policy or procedure to improve their practice performance.

The initiative is evidence of a technology transfer between the UK and the US. There are clear and acknowledged links between the Massachusetts initiative and 'community social work' (Barclay 1982), which originated in the UK in the late 1970s and early 1980s. Themes common to both include:

- using teamwork as a model for working and problem solving with the community;
- locally based practice – typically community social work teams should cover small geographical areas with populations of approximately 5,000 to 10,000;
- an emphasis on informal knowledge of neighbourhoods and communities;
- a belief that service users are not 'clients' or dependants of the system – they are recognised as potential assets to their communities and their need for supplemental support reflects only one aspect of their lives;
- the accessibility of public social services at times when families can use them;
- the prevention of problems arising in neighbourhoods and communities by creating opportunities for individuals and families to grow in healthy and constructive ways: 'multiple domains of family development from education and health care, to good after-school programming, recreation and celebration must be addressed if families are to achieve long term outcomes related to genuine well-being' (US Department of Health and Human Services Children's Bureau 2000: 10–11);

- encouraging the participation of the residents in the 'patch' or neighbourhood in the programme or initiative;
- respecting the diversity of individuals, families and neighbourhoods.

The strategies which created the Massachusetts Patch initiative were based on these principles and emerged from negotiations with key stakeholders and constituencies complementary to these principles. In order to work on the complex agenda described by these principles, Patch has to operate on a number of levels simultaneously: the neighbourhood team, the Patch community council and the administrative council.

Patch councils are diverse bodies composed of community leaders or elders. They include service users and service providers who want to play a role and contribute something to the community. The administrative team is composed of area office directors, area programme managers and family support specialists (drawn from statutory and voluntary agencies and organisations). This team focuses on problem solving at the policy level.

Before outlining how the combined insights and practice expertise – gained through the application of community social work methodology and principles to an American child welfare innovation – might be assimilated into a new model for Irish family support services, it is useful to examine the contribution that the Australian focus on the intangible benefits of social capital might equally bring to this process.

The Australian Contribution to a New Model

The essence of the Australian contribution is that it makes clear the importance of linking family support service development with the generation of social capital in the task of actively promoting the welfare of children who are not receiving adequate care and attention. According to Bullen and Onyx's research (1999) into the role and importance of social capital for family support work in New South Wales:

1. Social capital is measurable in local communities and the general social capital factor has at least eight elements falling into two broad groups. Table 5.5 sets out the measurable elements of social capital.

TABLE 5.5: ELEMENTS OF SOCIAL CAPITAL

Arenas	Capacity Building Blocks
Participation in local community	Pro-activity in a social context
Neighbourhood connection	Feelings of trust and safety
Family and friends connections	Tolerance of diversity
Work connections	Value of life

Source: Bullen, P. and Onyx, J. (1999), *Social Capital: Family Support Services and Neighbourhood and Community Centres in New South Wales,* Sydney: Family Support Services Association of NSW.

2. The data suggests that family support service users surveyed in the study increased their levels of social capital over the time they were receiving services.

3. The data suggests a possible progression in the use of services, with users' initial involvement in domiciliary individualised services beginning a process of developing the human capital necessary for them to participate in groups run by family support services. In these groups, further skills and confidence are developed as well as connections with group participants and the wider community. Successful experience in family support groups enables these users to connect with other community organisations and, in turn, these expanded organisations enable more neighbourhood and community connections to be made and thus further the generation of greater levels of social capital.

The UK Contribution to a New Model

The recommendations of the Seebohm Report (1968), which led to the establishment of local authority social work departments, were grounded in a commitment to enhancing social citizenship as well as tackling the problems of society through state intervention guided by professionally trained social workers. This institutionalised commitment to the community dimension of welfare practices has been realised, albeit on a limited and patchy basis, by social services departments operating from a community social work perspective and crafting social inclusion agendas resting on concepts of empowerment and partnership. The practice theory which has grown up around this strand of social work provides a template for developing intervention strategies and programmes like Homestart and Surestart, which attempt to realise community well-being in addition to individual welfare.

A New Model

Figure 5.1 illustrates a new model of community-oriented family support practice.

CONCLUSION

This chapter describes how family support practice repertoires have been shaped and governed by historical issues and organisational imperatives in Ireland and beyond. It advances a new model for family support practice in Ireland, which draws on US, Australian and UK practice theories and is influenced by reflective practice and civic renewal themes. The next chapter puts the case forward for policy intervention to secure community development and family support outcomes, which produce social capital.

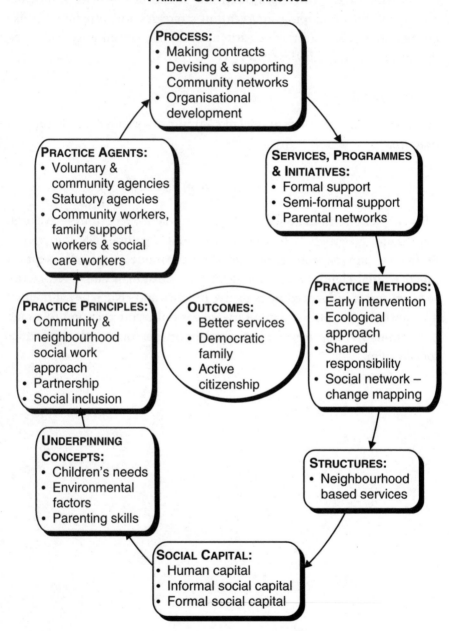

FIGURE 5.1: NEW MODEL FOR COMMUNITY-ORIENTED
FAMILY SUPPORT PRACTICE

CHAPTER SIX

VERIFYING THE STORY

INTRODUCTION

If social capital is an intangible social resource that can be enjoyed by all citizens, then it has public policy implications. Policies are usually associated with objectives. However, in order to assess the usefulness of a policy objective, it is necessary to see whether the outcomes of policy are consistent with the objectives. In simple terms: has it done what it was supposed to do?

So, can policies which create social capital be used in Irish communities to promote social cohesion and social inclusion? Can the effects of social capital policy making be measured on the ground? More interestingly, if it can be measured then, in policy terms, methods can be selected to ensure that it is managed and operationalised. Areas addressed in this chapter include:

- Social capital in everyday life.
- Activating a social capital policy model.
- Manifesting active citizenship.
- Developing policy – the Camden story.
- Measuring the 'social glue' in neighbourhoods, communities and wider society.

SOCIAL CAPITAL IN EVERYDAY LIFE

People did not live in Ireland then. They lived in small intense communities which often varied greatly in spirit and character over the course of even a few miles.

John McGahern, *Memoir*

In his memoir McGahern invites the reader to connect up the details of social capital formation and the divergent levels of spirit and character to be found in different communities. He provides us with a stylish literary account of the quality of social relations in Ireland in the recent past. His work helps us to understand the social circumstances which pattern the lives of individuals and communities. However, McGahern was not charged with the responsibility of taking account of social capital formation and devising and implementing social policies which could potentially reduce or increase levels of social capital in neighbourhoods, communities and wider society. Empirical investigation of social capital, conducted with validity and reliability, and linked to theoretical understandings of the concept is essential for the development of an explicit social capital strategy at micro, meso and macro social levels. The challenge for policy makers and professionals who wish to apply the concept in practice is to develop a measurement framework which is sufficiently rigorous and robust to uncover the complexities of various forms of social capital. As Cummins points out:

> While defining social capital is in itself notoriously difficult, measuring it and tracking changes in it is no easier. One of the inherent difficulties is that the phrase 'social capital' has no intrinsic meaning to the vast majority of people. This makes it impossible to question people directly about its presence or absence in their lives. To further complicate matters, social capital is not one concept but a bundle of different attributes that refers to such things as trust, reciprocity and community cohesion. Each of these concepts in turn is very complex, and measuring the degree to which each is present in a community means using several different yardsticks. As a result, there is no single measure of social capital that can be reliably used. (2006: 31)

Single item measures of social capital produce limited data. According to Cummins, minimum data levels have been achieved by single item measurement strategies such as:

- dropping stamped addressed letters in the streets of different neighbourhoods and tracking how many are posted;
- leaving wallets in local areas and seeing how many arrive at the police station or are returned to their owners;
- using proxies such as voter turnout or participation in volunteering.

Because these strategies rely too heavily on chance factors and use indicators that mean different things to different people, such as volunteering, they yield one-dimensional data which is of restricted worth in informing social policy interventions.

An important part of the policy making and intervention is evaluation – did the policy intervention have the anticipated effect, and at what price? This question applies not only to policy interventions directly targeted at increasing social capital, but also to those that are directed towards achieving different outcomes but that might have unintended consequences for social capital.

ACTIVATING A SOCIAL CAPITAL CENTRED POLICY MODEL

Table 6.1 details the span of social capital policy making.

The Case for Active Policy Intervention

Evidence that social capital is declining is a major source of concern for nations, including Ireland. The nature of Irish society has altered over the past twenty years and the social glue created by families, extended families, faith based communities and many of the large-scale national voluntary, sporting and cultural organisations has been diluted to such an extent that it needs to be reinvigorated. Across the world, policy makers are recognising the dynamic relationship between social capital, economic growth, health, crime and the efficacy of government (Ahern 2005; OECD 2001; NESF 2003).

TABLE 6.1: A SOCIAL CAPITAL POLICY CONTINUUM

Social Capital Insensitive
Social capital is neglected or ignored in poorly designed policy making processes. At the very least, social capital is not served or supported and at worst it is reduced.

Social Capital Sensitive
Social capital receives 'lipservice' as policies and practices for various societal sectors (education, health) are developed. Social capital is mentioned or presumed impacts upon it are described in general or vague terms.

Social Capital Focused
Social capital is not merely mentioned. A formal social capital audit or policy proofing mechanism monitoring outcome and policy instruments on health, crime, welfare etc. is established.

Social Capital Supportive
The explicit goal is to enable social capital formation through policies which encourage capacity building blocks to surface at micro, meso and macro social levels.

Social Capital Centred
Social capital becomes the centre of attention in a cross-cutting policy framework aimed at stimulating active citizenship and civic renewal.

However, as Jordan (2007) makes clear, some forms of social capital create costs for society. Where marginalised communities feel excluded from the mainstream by virtue of ethnicity, faith or income, bonding social capital may have unintended consequences and drive a wedge between social groups by reinforcing identities which reject other groups or the whole culture. As Halpern puts it:

> Since different forms of social capital have differential impacts on different policy outcomes, a social capital framework does not relieve us of decisions over what our relative priorities are. For example, economic growth appears to be particularly affected by macro level, bridging, norm-based social capital, while health is particularly affected by micro level, bonding, network-based social capital. Officials responsible for delivering a strong economy and those responsible for delivering public health will not necessarily agree on the same social capital programme. (2005: 288–289)

With Halpern's (2005: 35) 'vitamin model' of social ca[...]
less likelihood of a particular policy promoting one kind of [...]
at the expense of another. A blend of vitamins promotes well-
dividuals and healthy and valuable communities are nurtured by a blend
of different types of social capital. Policy measures should avoid displac-
ing existing forms of social capital. Ideally, bonding social capital should
not be forfeited in return for bridging capital. Integrated community
development strategies can deliver:

- human capital – through formal and informal education
  programmes;
- bonding capital – through membership of clubs, groups and
  associations;
- bridging capital – through the creation of channels for cross-
  cultural contact and employment opportunities;
- linking social capital – through a collective approach to accessing resources.

Circumstances may occasionally arise which justify the forfeiture of a
particular form of social capital in order to sustain a new policy direction
and to assist in the formation of new and more dynamic forms of social
capital. A policy of re-housing inner city residents in new peripheral estates on the edge of towns and cities will improve the quality of accommodation available to the residents but will probably bring to an end
the close-knit community they have created for themselves. The bonding
capital accumulated by residents over a lengthy period is in danger of being lost in this policy process. Improving the physical environment has
been prioritised over the maintenance of the social environment. However, as we have seen in the previous chapter, a positive commitment to
generating social capital through community development strategies can,
if properly planned for, reduce the risk of community networks being
harmed by this re-settlement policy. On a basic level, adequate physical
infrastructure should be in position before residents occupy their new accommodation. Playgrounds, parks, shops, meeting rooms, schools, transport services, childcare and other basic amenities such as sports facilities
are pre-requisites. Educational, cultural and social networks can be fostered under the auspices of a family centre or community centre and be a
focal point for human capital formation.

Unintended Consequences of Policy

Because the promotion of social capital depends on actors other than the state's own agents, policy makers rely on partners, intermediaries and civil society to assist in the process. But policy which acts at a distance in this way can be misinterpreted or activated in unanticipated ways. Furedi (2002) points out that policies designed to promote volunteering run the risk of degrading the meaning of volunteering, as the existence of some form of reward removes the element of altruism and channels people into doing something more out of self-interest than from a desire to serve others. Field provides further examples of unintended consequences:

> A policy aimed at promoting volunteering by providing funds to voluntary bodies may end up by encouraging competition rather than co-operation among those who are applying for funds, and displacing civic activists with paid professionals. Policies designed to mobilise voluntary bodies as service delivery agents may inadvertently suppress their capacity to nurture social capital. (2003: 120)

Fukuyama (2001) warns that excessive state intervention can have an unconstructive impact on social capital and may even interfere with the freedom of individuals. However, he acknowledges that governments may well institute policies to surmount some forms of negative social capital. Examples of this might include state action to eliminate certain behaviours which sustain economic inefficiency. Targets to be eliminated include cronyism and cartels in the business world, or the use of networks to favour the careers of a particular privileged ethnic group or gender. While public support would probably be forthcoming for policies combating the negative effects of social capital generated in this way, state involvement should be kept to a minimum and the task of creating social capital should be left to the initiative of individuals. Other examples of possible unintended outcomes might involve some women's rights being compromised by policies targeting social capital generation (Molyneaux 2002), and a policy of substituting active citizenship for state support may intentionally or unintentionally lead to a reduction in state welfare services.

Social Capital Impact Statements

> Ireland currently has a number of policy-proofing and impact assessment mechanisms and processes relating to poverty, health, environment, equality, gender and regulatory change. In some instances, these mechanisms and processes have led the way to change at the broader EU level; in others, they have come about as a result of the requirements of the EU institutions. (Corrigan 2006: 44)

Active policy intervention might be assisted by the introduction of social capital policy proofing into the policy making of government departments. This would compel those designing public policy to consider the impact of these policies on social capital formation.

ACTIVE CITIZENSHIP

Task Force on Active Citizenship

The establishment of a Task Force on Active Citizenship in 2005 by Taoiseach Bertie Ahern was a welcome development as it has the potential to re-focus policy making on the importance of active citizens and healthy communities. In Celtic Tiger Ireland the main thrust of policy making has been primarily associated with the securing of traditional 'hard' outcomes, such as increasing gross domestic product, often to the detriment of the overall social fabric. However, there is a growing consensus that viewing all policy choices through a wealth creation lens has resulted in a degradation of the policy process itself. While Bertie Ahern's government has declared that the quality of life in society and the ultimate health of our communities depends on the willingness of people to become involved and active, its policies have, arguably, taken Irish society in a direction that makes it more and more unlikely that people can or will be actively engaged in contributing to the common good. People's happiness has not increased in line with their wealth and whole sections of society have gained no economic benefits from these policies but have experienced a sharp decline in their quality of life. In her forensic examination of the impact of policies which are singularly attached to wealth generation and maximising consumption, Dr Elizabeth Cullen (2006) lays bare the threat to social cohesion which such policies pose. In a society where notions of citizenship are bound up with the acquisition of money, it may be unrealistic to expect people to put this to one side when it comes to active citizenship. Financial gain attributed to partnership policies is, under present policy arrangements, leading to the privatisation of the traditionally public collective domains of education and health. Policies promoting privatised health care and privatised education are undercutting social solidarity and, as such, they are major barriers to active citizenship.

Policies that place well-being before wealth generation, such as those outlined in the Department of Health and Children publication *Quality and Fairness – A Health System for You* (2001), are stillborn, while policies that have encouraged individual profiteering – section 23 tax shelters on properties, for example – are omnipresent. Sequestering of socially cohesive policy initiatives in turn places the onus for social capital formation back on individuals who are struggling to cope with an increasingly one-dimensional citizenship. One-dimensional citizenship offers limited labour market choices and limited or poor public services, while those who profiteer from the deregulated housing and property market can choose the terms of their income, their children's education and their own health and welfare. This social contract does not encourage voluntarism. However it does promote an increasingly segmented society; a society which appears not to subscribe to the belief that together we are better and where volunteers and active citizens appear to be propping up the public educational system, the public health and welfare system and public cultural, recreational and sporting activities, while the better-off beneficiaries of tax shelters and property speculation can, as Giddens puts it, opt out of mainstream society altogether:

> Two forms of exclusion are becoming marked in contemporary societies. One is the exclusion of those at the bottom, cut off from the mainstream of opportunities society has to offer. At the top is voluntary exclusion, the 'revolt of the elites': a withdrawal from public institutions on the part of more affluent groups, who choose to live separately from the rest of the society. Privileged groups start to live in fortress communities, and pull out from public education and public health systems. (1998: 103)

Given these social circumstances, the way forward for active citizenship on the macro level is to:

- re-orient the policy process away from policy programmes which undermine social cohesion;
- engage in policy making which promotes civil renewal.

Active Citizenship, Social Capital and Civil Renewal

Social capital is an intangible resource for active citizens engaged in civil renewal processes. The Putnam endorsed perspective on social capital – 'social cohesion is produced by three primary features of social life (networks, norms, trust) that enable participants to act together more effectively to pursue shared objectives' (O'Doherty 2006: 31) – is an important facilitator of active citizenship and civil renewal. Network formation creates entry points for drawing people into formal and informal volunteering, thereby creating levels of trust that are needed for communities to work together. When trust is created, people are more inclined to help others, especially if they trust other people in their community to participate too, either directly or indirectly. However, trust is another victim of the passage from producer to consumer society which has taken place in Ireland during the boom years. Consumerism legitimises and prizes individuality and relationships which produce reciprocal trust are supplanted by relationships between a customer and the market. As Bauman states:

> Producers can fulfil their vocation only collectively; production is a collective endeavour, it presumes the division of tasks, co-operation of actors and co-ordination of their activities … . Producers are together even when they act apart. The work of each one can only gain from more inter-individual communication, harmony and integration.
>
> Consumers are just the opposite. Consumption is a thoroughly individual, solitary and, in the end, lonely activity; an activity which is fulfilled by quenching and arousing, assuaging and whipping up a desire which is always private, and not easily communicable sensation. There is no such thing as collective consumption. (2005: 30)

Civil renewal can take place anywhere but, when it is underpinned by measures designed to assist social capital formation, it empowers marginalised communities to build on this social capital and become active citizens who are engaged both in improving their local communities and in participating in mainstream civic life.

MANIFESTING ACTIVE CITIZENSHIP

Crafting an Authentic Agenda

In the authentic version of active citizenship, inequality is tackled and democracy is re-invigorated through empowering communities to take charge of their own regeneration and renewal. A twofold process is required to make a difference on the ground.

Step One – Re-inventing Volunteering

A sense of duty propels people into voluntary activity. Making fulfilment of duty attractive in a society where a supreme value is accorded to the right to enjoy the profits of private enterprise is not going to be easy. The values of a market-driven economy where both partners work are not compatible with having the time or moral courage to give to the community. Impetus for a reinvigorated volunteering dimension to citizenship can be generated if the proposition that people's social networks are a valuable national asset is accepted by the government and manifested through policies that acknowledge the importance of different kinds of voluntary activity.

Civic Service Volunteers

Civic service volunteers are engaged in needed public work, promoting social justice and creating opportunities which advance cross-cultural understanding. Civic service volunteers are frequently called upon to initiate and organise responses to unmet social needs which are not being addressed by mainstream service provision. Frequently, this kind of volunteering approximates to a full-time job. For example, a volunteer on the board of management of a school or family centre is charged with the same responsibilities as any employer in terms of recruiting and managing staff, and financial control. Civic service volunteers find themselves plugging the gaps in the state's social protection frameworks. Their efforts prevent the social fabric unravelling. However, civic service volunteers should be complementing direct public service provision rather than substituting for it. The pivotal role of civic service volunteers as stakeholders in the upkeep of indispensable social services can be recognised by:

- giving tax credits to people who engage in voluntary civic service at local, national, international and transnational levels in the following arenas – boards of managements of schools, community centres/family support centres, overseas community development programmes, youth work, older citizens agencies/organisations, special needs agencies/organisations etc.;
- giving time off work to people who engage in voluntary civic service;
- giving career recognition to people who engage in voluntary civic service;
- providing training and education opportunities for people who engage in voluntary civic service;
- providing educational credits for students engaging in voluntary civic service.

Cultural and Recreational Volunteers

Participating in cultural and recreational activities with other people can help to overcome barriers of mistrust which impede the formation of social capital. Research exists which indicates that people who participate in culture and recreational activities are also more likely to participate in society in other ways (Robson 2003). This kind of voluntary activity can be achieved through the creation of participation ladders which facilitate movement through a series of steps:

1. Involvement as a cultural or recreational 'doer' – somebody who takes part in cultural and/or recreational activities.
2. Involvement as a cultural or recreational volunteer – helping to run or organise cultural and/or recreational activities.
3. Involvement as a cultural or recreational leader – helping to lead and govern cultural organisations and determine priorities for cultural and recreational provision and/or spending.

However, it should be noted that there are qualitative differences between voluntary effort focused on hard-to-reach groups (marginalised young people, immigrants, socially excluded communities, the disabled) and voluntary work with large-scale mainstream, semi-commercialised bodies (GAA, Galway Arts Festival). Participation in mainstream cultural and/or recreational voluntary activities is attractive because it boosts credentialed human capital levels (thereby enhancing career prospects) through social and leisure networks. By comparison, the return on voluntary effort with hard-to-reach groups in present day Ireland is meagre. Measures encouraging this strand of volunteering are:

- time off work to people who engage in cultural and/or recreational volunteering with hard-to-reach groups;
- career recognition to people who engage in cultural and/or recreational volunteering with hard-to-reach groups;
- training and education opportunities for people who engage in cultural and/or recreational volunteering with hard-to-reach groups;
- providing educational credits for students engaging in cultural and/or recreational volunteering with hard-to-reach groups.

Step Two – 'Opening up' Government to Provide Opportunities for Participation in Decision Making

As Lowndes (2005) has pointed out, participation can be seen as a two-way process, with a supply side – empowered citizens with the desire and capacity to participate – and a demand side – flexible and responsive government that is open to and encouraging of, participation. If citizens do not have the skills and confidence to engage with the opportunities for participation that do exist, then it is all too likely that these opportunities will become dominated by unrepresentative minorities. However, even the most motivated and engaged citizens will quickly become cynical and disillusioned if they come to see consultation and engagement as mere 'box ticking' exercises that have no real impact on government. (Keaney 2006)

Ireland, in common with other European welfare states, is under pressure 'from above' and 'below' to revitalise active forms of citizenship. The challenge from above is associated with the expanding field of transnational governance. Both the European Union (EU) and the Organisation for Economic Co-operation and Development (OECD) have emphasised the need for member states to move from 'passive' to 'active' policies promoting labour market participation as the primary goal of social protection schemes. Adequate and secure income support should only be made available to those who are incapable of working. The challenge from below is how to respond to the complex changes brought about by a trend towards individualisation and the loss of traditions in late-modern societies (see Chapter One). Citizens are no longer willing to accept a 'top down' bureaucratic or paternalistic mode of administration setting the welfare agenda and they are opposed to rigid and inflexible social protection measures which are framed around the arbitrary exercise of discretionary powers. This pressure provides greater scope for a participatory welfare state and underscores governance which encourages broad participation in decision making.

The governance dimension of active citizenship, as a desirable collective outcome, concerns the contribution of social capital to the realisation of wider public policy objectives and outcomes. Just as active citizenship does not exist in isolation from other areas of public policy, social capital formation and civic renewal cannot proceed in isolation from other public policies. Better integration and co-ordination between the different parts of government towards a public policy outcome has eluded successive Irish governments. Hence the Government needs to open up opportunities for people to participate in a process of civil renewal. A new method of governing is the key to activating citizens to participate in shaping their social environments. A shift to governance reflects a move away from top-down, centralised government towards a new process of governing based on bargaining, negotiation and other types of exchanges rather than through diktat.

> Governance is a recognition that, because even the full exercise of state powers in many areas cannot guarantee the outcomes sought, more progress is made (with less wastage of resources on surveillance, enforcement and other transaction costs) when all the parties whose actions constitute part of the needed response co-operate with the manner in which their diverse contributions are to be governed in order to reach the desired outcomes. (NESC 2005: 207)

A significant policy reform, which shifts the balance of government effort towards genuine civic renewal by ensuring that people have the resources and ability to associate together, thereby focusing more on policies to build civic skills and capacity, is the desired outcome. A new governance structure, underpinned by a key integrative mechanism will:

- at a local level, implement policies that encourage people to get together and form networks;
- strengthen community ownership of public assets such as family support centres;
- build local social capital through urban and rural planning strategies which bring people together, e.g. creation of public spaces and amenities where people can meet and form relationships;
- strengthen social capital, at regional or national level, by encouraging joint working between voluntary, community and state organisations through coalitions and forums;
- put organisations with civil renewal agendas in touch with each other and encourage international as well as national networking and exchange.

Civic Renewal Centres

State sponsored locally integrated civic renewal centres with the following functions will provide the integrative mechanism required to translate the new active citizenship policies into practice:

- Charting the voluntary and community efforts of individuals. Individuals will be registered as volunteers or community activists and levels of engagement will be logged.
- Each centre will have a responsibility to build capacity through skills, structures and support. This will involve promoting lifelong learning, enabling the development of citizenship education for young people through strategies similar to those employed by the UK Learning and Skills Development Agencys' Post-16 Citizenship Development programme. This educational qualification for young people is intended to recognise achievement in active citizenship. Delivered through the mainstream post-16 education and training system (further education colleges, learning and skills development agency), it is structured around candidates

preparing for, taking action on, and evaluating a citizenship issue. Established in 2006, it is a national programme which seeks to give young people the knowledge, skills and understanding to play an effective role in society at local, national and international levels.

- Releasing the social dividend – through authorising tax credits, time off work, and implementing educational and training programmes for active citizens registered with centres.

Report of the Task Force on Active Citizenship

The Task Force on Active Citizenship was established to advise the Government on the steps that can be taken to ensure that the wealth of civic spirit and active participation already present in Ireland continues to grow and develop. Published in March 2007, the report makes some worthwhile recommendations to government covering the following areas:

- participation in the democratic process;
- the public service and citizens;
- community engagement and promoting a sense of community;
- education for citizenship;
- ethnic and cultural diversity and the challenge of engaging newcomers.

However, it does not address the policy formation which is frustrating the active citizenship agenda. Overall, the report raises some interesting questions about the social contract between the citizen and the state. Some of the 'barriers' to active citizenship which are mentioned in the report include:

- new housing developments which are not taking account of the needs of the people and communities for transport, common areas, open spaces and community facilities. In this context, the report suggests, it is difficult for people to feel respected or included or to inculcate a sense of community or citizenship – there is a need for reform of local government and planning.

- there is a cynicism and a lack of confidence in democratic and some other consultative structures, particularly at local level, with individuals and organisations not feeling that they are genuinely listened to and this is exacerbated by the focus in public services on customers rather than citizens.

Government support for active citizenship has the potential to become a key strategy for developing new skills among citizens and for creating the kind of community empowerment and culture of self-help and mutual support that is a springboard for civic renewal. In order to progress this strategy, a suite of new policies that directly stimulate social capital formation must supplant present policies, which are actively reducing social capital levels amongst the population.

DEVELOPING POLICY – THE CAMDEN STORY

Camden local authority in London has recognised the need for engaging in policy making which solves problems rather than applies solutions. To this end, they are committed to a role of 'place shaping', i.e. moving the emphasis from providing services to a broader role of advancing the well-being of a community and its citizens through social capital formation. This policy approach is informed by the results of a social capital measurement initiative undertaken by Camden.

In 2002 and 2005 the London Borough of Camden commissioned two surveys aimed at measuring social capital. Camden Council sought to understand the nature and degree of social capital existing at a neighbourhood level in the borough. Moving beyond the generalised arguments which connect high levels of social capital to a whole range of desirable social outcomes, Camden Council recognised that:

- 'If local government is to fulfil its wider community leadership role, it needs to consider social capital. This means that councils need to move beyond measuring their effectiveness just in terms of narrow service delivery. Emptying the bins on time and keeping the streets clean are, of course, important concerns. Failure to provide these basics affects people's lives and leads them to question what they are getting in return for their taxes. On its own, however, excellence in the field of public service delivery will not build strong communities. The Government is now asking councils to broaden their horizons and concern themselves with community well-being in a much more ambitious sense.

- ... local councils are also especially well placed to help nurture social capital – simply because they are the tier of the state closest to people's daily lives. Social capital is very locally rooted. It relates to one's relationships with neighbours, local clubs and societies, and frontline public services. Local authorities are therefore uniquely placed within the public sector to work with local communities, to foster the development of social capital.'

(Muir 2006: 8–10)

Getting Practical in Camden

Having been responsible for some negative decision making in relation to social capital in the past (e.g. slum clearances and tower block development in the 1950s and 1960s, which had a negative impact on existing social relations), Camden Council intends to pro-actively nurture a vibrant civil life. Despite its upbeat approach, the Council is not blind to the limitations of its role in this regard. It cannot easily counteract the historical factors that have driven variation in social capital accumulation over time. Over periods of time, class structure, social mobility, levels of educational attainment and degrees of civic activism have influenced the opportunities available to individuals to accumulate social capital. Rebalancing these underlying factors is a long-term project for any local government structure.

Local authorities such as Camden are also restrained by their obligation to defer to the choices made by the public and cannot create, for example, an active residents' association or ensure that young people will be diverted from anti-social behaviour through the provision of some new sports equipment.

Lessons Learnt

The general lessons learnt from Camden Council's two surveys are set out below:

1. If local authorities are convinced of the importance of social capital then they ought to observe and measure it in the neighbourhoods that they serve.

2. After this, they must establish the conditions for social capital formation through service delivery. How can a local authority go about performing its core service functions in a way which maximises opportunities for creating social capital? Camden Council have employed the following three strategies in order to establish better conditions for social capital formation: a) using public space to create stronger social networks – 'One existing example in Camden is the Boulevard Project, which aims to replace existing footways, design out anti-social behaviour, improve shop frontages and remove unnecessary obstacles from the street scene, to make the street a more attractive place to spend time. This type of approach could be taken further by incorporating social capital concerns more fully into planning and design policies, for instance by encouraging communal gardens and wider pavements' (Muir 2006: 21); b) establishing connections between people through consultation. For example, in a novel approach to consultation, residents were consulted about new shrub and tree planting in their streets whilst taking part in a walkabout with council officers. These walkabouts offered residents an opportunity to meet their neighbours; c) working with young people – Camden's Family in Focus schemes have worked on the development of opportunities for local residents and council teams to produce programmes designed to bring young people and their parents together to resolve day-to-day problems. Programme activities such as gardening projects, residential courses for young people to develop confidence and social skills, family trips and community fun days have been particularly useful on estates where anti-social behaviour has been a concern.

3. In addition to a traditional service delivery role, a local authority should have a public voice and a community leadership role which actively enhances the growth of bridging and bonding social capital between its citizens. In 2005, Camden

Council presented its Exceptional People in Camden awards to volunteers who had been working hard in the community. It also considered setting funding criteria for cultural events which would stipulate that such events must be designed to bring people from different communities together in order to promote bridging social capital.

MEASURING THE STICKINESS OF THE 'SOCIAL GLUE' IN NEIGHBOURHOODS, COMMUNITIES AND WIDER SOCIETY

At the heart of policy making that embraces the idea of promoting social capital lies the challenge of measurement. However social capital is a multi-dimensional concept and, in order to understand the nature of the interaction between the separate dimensions of social capital, we must first conceptualise social capital's dimensions in separate terms. Measuring social capital at all levels (micro, meso and macro) and in all its forms and types enables policy makers to calculate the impact of policy approaches and proposals on a range of social outcomes (health, crime, economic performance). Across a range of policy areas, but particularly in the area of community development, funding tends to follow evidence of what can be shown to work and what can be shown to be effective.

In November 2001, the UK Office for National Statistics in collaboration with the Home Office began a process of developing a set of harmonised questions which could be used in local and national surveys. A review of the literature demonstrated that many government surveys included questions on social capital but that a variety of approaches were being used to measure it. The use of an assortment of measurement methods was responsible for an overall lack of cohesion between data sets and variation in concepts and definitions. An inter-departmental Social Capital Working Group was established 'to agree a definition of social capital for use across government departments, to develop a framework for its measurement, and develop a set of fully tested questions consistent with this definition and framework. The work was split into three stages:

1. agreement of an operational definition;
2. development of a framework for measurement;
3. development and testing of questions.'
    (Harper and Kelly 2003: 2)

The definition employed by the Organisation for Economic Co-operation and Development – 'social capital has been defined variously by different researchers, but is here taken to include the networks, norms, values and understandings that facilitate co-operation within or among groups'(OECD 2001) – was adopted for use across government departments.

The task to be completed during the second stage was to set out which specific dimensions of social capital should be measured, provide a framework for analysing the concept and thereby develop a harmonised set of questions (stage three). Stage two began with an investigation of previously developed frameworks, indicators and questions. Four frameworks for measuring social capital – used in the 2001 Home Office Citizenship Survey (see Attwood *et al.* 2003), Blaxter *et al.* 2001, General Household Survey 2001 and Health Survey for England 2000 – were identified and used to create a survey matrix. The intention was to highlight social capital questions used in surveys and group these according to social capital dimensions. Objective and subjective indicators for measuring each dimension were incorporated into the UK framework. A harmonised set of questions for each dimension was developed in stage three (see Appendix B for the full harmonised question set). Because the harmonised question set was designed to take no more than twenty minutes to administer, only a small number of indicators could be explored in survey interviews:

> Due to the time restrictions, the set was confined to those indicators considered central to social capital. It can be used in its entirety or, if only one dimension is of interest, only the questions relating to that dimension may be used. (Harper and Kelly 2003: 10)

The Office for National Statistics' harmonised question set has been used in the UK General Household Survey and an adapted and abridged version was used by O'Doherty and Farrelly (2006) in a survey of social capital and changing settlement patterns in two villages in County Kerry. Table 6.2 sets out the UK social capital measurement framework.

Community Spirit in Dublin

Dublin City Council recently surveyed more than 400 people in Dublin in a similar attempt to map out levels of social capital across the city. The research into factors affecting social cohesion in Dublin City has

TABLE 6.2: UK SOCIAL CAPITAL MEASUREMENT FRAMEWORK

Dimension	Examples of Indicators
Social participation:	• Number of cultural, leisure, social groups involved in and frequency and intensity of involvement. • Volunteering: frequency and intensity of involvement • Religious activity
Civic participation:	• Perceptions of ability to influence events • Knowledge about local and national affairs • Contact with public officials or public representatives • Involvement with local action groups • Propensity to vote
Social networks and social support:	• Frequency of seeing and speaking to relatives, friends, neighbours • Extent of virtual networks and frequency of contact • Number of close friends and relatives who live nearby • Exchange of help • Perceived control and satisfaction with life
Reciprocity and trust:	• Trust in other people who are like you • Trust in other people who are not like you • Confidence in institutions at different levels • Doing favours and vice versa • Perception of shared values
Views of the local area:	• Views on physical environment • Facilities in the area • Enjoyment of living in the area • Fear of crime

Source: Harper, R. and Kelly, M. (2003), *Measuring Social Capital in the United Kingdom,* London: United Kingdom Office for National Statistics.

shown that fewer people are getting involved in the community and that overall there appears to be a decline in community spirit. Commissioned as part of an initiative by Dublin City Council to increase levels of social capital across the city, the research has indicated that social cohesion in less well-off communities have benefited from investment in facilities, refurbishment projects and the establishment of new community groups. More middle income areas have witnessed a decline in social cohesion due to factors such as lack of time, family responsibilities, work patterns and changing values. The research report recommends the implementation of a range of initiatives to rekindle community ties across the city. Initiatives include:

- encouraging businesses to engage with their local communities and share their assets and resources;
- setting up a 'neighbourhood link system' to unite people who share the same interests;
- ensuring that the city council builds on the assets and resources of local areas rather than adopting the traditional deficit approach to problem-solving;
- identifying a set of basic values for community living and ensuring that these are adopted by city authorities;
- introducing voter education programmes and active citizenship classes in schools;
- setting up a new community liaison and development unit in the city council in order to promote the social inclusion of newcomers and ethnic minorities.

CONCLUSION

National and local governments, using empirical evidence, can apply concepts and understandings of social capital in their policies and practices. Their role as 'place makers' is to build not just the physical fabric of communities but the social fabric as well. However, there is a danger that policy making can be subverted by the short-term nature of the political process and that social cohesion as a desirable outcome becomes reliant on 'sticking plaster' solutions rather than longer-term commitments to increasing the social glue factor in society.

CONCLUSION

CREATING NEW STORIES

NEW WORK FOR NEW TIMES

Work came to be confined to the type of activity which can be entered into business books; that is the kind of work which can be sold and bought, has an exchange value recognized in the market and so can command monetary remuneration. The work ethic chimed in with concentrated and unchallenged discrimination: staying outside the labour market, doing unsold or unsellable labour meant, in the language of the work ethic, being unemployed and that meant non-work. The consequences of all this are in many respects disastrous. They contribute heavily to the gradual yet relentless falling apart of community and neighbourhood bonds, of that social cohesion whose maintenance is after all a tremendously time-, labour- and skill-consuming activity. (Bauman 2005: 119)

To paraphrase Bauman, in a world populated by consumers there is no room for a welfare state and in the world of the welfare claimant there is little or no room for consumerism. Welfare claimants are flawed or non-consumers and are excluded from mainstream networks of social interactions and exchanges. 'Consumer' is defined currently as a cultural identity (something that is owned by a person as an attitude or attribute). There is a real danger that active citizenship and the values and cultural practices associated with it will be reduced to a branding exercise.

The starting point for this book was a recognition that supporting the family as a social welfare institution is a prerequisite for the development of a new social contract where order maintenance and normative regulation are sustained through active citizenship, self-help and mutuality. The principal social role currently allocated to Irish families, under the influence of affluence, is to connect with the responsibilities attached to them as consumers. The challenge facing family support practitioners and policy makers is to re-engage them as producers of collective welfare. Social care practitioners are uniquely positioned, through their expanding professional project, to nurture, support and sustain the intangible resources in people's lives. The new model for community-oriented family support practice proposed in this book takes account of best practice operating here in Ireland and abroad. In order for active citizenship to replace reactive citizenship, relationships and networks reinforcing consumer and claimant identity forms must be reforged.

What is required to achieve the objective of active citizenship is a culture-changing government. The key challenge for government is to identify new governance strategies with which it can seek to persuade and enable the general public to change its culture. The critical policy areas requiring new governance structures are:

- Work-Life Balance
    - Family-friendly policies.
    - Corporate social responsibility.
    - Life balance and spirituality.

- Lifelong Learning
    - Human and social capital.
    - Supportive networks for learning.
    - Further and higher education.
    - Citizenship education.

- Spatial Planning
    - Balanced development.
    - Built and natural environment.
    - Civic communities' associational networks.

- Supporting Community and Voluntary Organisations
  - Community involvement in government initiatives.
  - Recognition for the time, labour and skill invested by volunteers in maintaining social cohesion.

- Corporate Citizenship
  - Placing a duty on commercial organisations to extend their role beyond making money to making a contribution to society.

However, individuals will not change their behaviour if they sense that they are being duped and are simply being drawn into a re-branding exercise. An active citizenship campaign, which is ultimately leading towards privatising welfare provision and placing the responsibility for social cohesion on hard pressed and ill-equipped communities, will not contribute to economic and social progress. This is where the two sides of the government's active citizenship are in some obvious tension with each other. The principles of 'strong, civic-minded, independent citizens' (Report of the Task Force 2007, Taoiseach's foreword) are grounded in a pragmatic, self-deterministic version of citizenship which is of a different quality to a citizenship issuing from a 'sense of loyalty and belonging, collective identity and commitment that springs from self-generated group activity for chosen ends' (Jordan 2007: 105). More holistic government is the key to developing an overall policy framework for fostering social capital formation. Holistic government – horizontal integration and partnership between citizens and state agencies – can provide a platform for civic renewal and ultimately make real inroads on establishing the symptoms and causes of social disorganisation.

An example of this approach can be seen in Camden Borough's creative approach to examining ways of promoting social cohesion which take account of the complex and changing nature of social capital. The story of the regeneration of Dublin docklands is another example of how a holistic approach to governance structures can foster the existing social capital of an area and strategically engage with the changes required to sustain and grow that social capital in the future. That there are similar projects being undertaken in the Shanakill Family Centre and the programme currently operating in Australia is evidence of a technology transfer in the area of social capital formation.

Such themes resonate with social care and social work's concerns about well-being and quality of life rather than material consumption or the work ethic.

This book has demonstrated how social care professionals, along with community development workers, social workers and youth workers can use their capacity building skills to progress this broader agenda – the promotion of well-being and quality of life – as they grapple with community problems of crime, unemployment, poor educational achievement and ill health.

Appendix A

Springboard Project Contact List 2005

Updated: February 2006

Name	Project	Address	Phone/Fax	e-mail	Managed by
Finola Halligan Project Leader	**Cherry Orchard**	Cherry Orchard Family Support Project, 21 Cherry Orchard Avenue, Cherry Orchard, Dublin 10	P: 01-6261985 F: 01-6261986	info@ cherryorchard. barnardos.ie finola. halligan@ barnardos.ie	Barnardos
Catherine Boonstra Project Leader	**Naas**	Naas Child and Family Project, 1 New Row, Newbridge Road, Naas, Co Kildare	P: 045-898623 F: as above	ncfp@kys.ie	Kildare Youth Services
Christine Farrell Project Leader	**Athlone**	Barnardos Child and Family Centre, 7 Ashdale, Coosan, Athlone, Co Westmeath	P: 090-6476422 F: 090-6476424	info@athlone. barnardos.ie christine. farrell@ barnardos.ie	Barnardos

155

Kathryn Delaney Project worker	**Tulla-more**	Barnardos Family Support Project, Patrick Street, Tullamore, Co Offaly	P: 0506-26803 F: 0506-20804	kathryn. delaney@ barnardos.ie	Barnardos
Marguerite McCormick Project Leader	**South-side**	Barnardos Family Support Project, 373 - 374 O'Malley Park, Southill, Limerick	P: 061-319290 F: 061-319291	info@southill. barnardos.ie marguerite. mccormick@ barnardos.ie	Barnardos
Olive Carter Project Leader	**Thurles**	Thurles Family Support & Day-care Service, The Mall House, Slievenamon Road, Thurles, Co Tipperary	P: 0504-20018 F: 0504-20019	info@thurles. barnardos.ie olive.carter@ thurles. barnardos.ie	Barnardos
Alice Malone Project Leader	**Muirhev-namor**	Muirhevnamor Springboard Initiative, c/o St Joseph's National School, Tom Bellew Avenue, Muirhevnamor, Dundalk, Co Louth	P: 042-9351680	muirhevnamor @esatclear.ie	Health Board
Karen Donlon Project Leader	**Navan**	Springboard Family Centre, CYWS Hall, Fair Green, Navan, Co Meath	P: 046-78221 046-78220 F: 046-78238	cyws@indigo. ie navspr@ indigo.ie	Limited Company
Paula Gorman Project Leader	**Sligo**	Resource House Project, 2 Racecourse View, Cranmore, Sligo	P: 07191-47070 F: as above	resource houseproject @eircom.net	Limited Company

Catherine Joyce Project Leader Una Conroy Project Co-ord	**Ballybeg**	Barnardos Family Support Project, 128 Clonard Park, Ballybeg, Waterford	P: 051-844140 F: 051-844141	info@ballybeg. barnardos.ie Catherine. joyce@bally- beg.barnardos. ie	Barnardos
Sarah Blows Project Leader	**Mahon**	Mahon Family Support Project, 8/9 Orchard View, Ringmahon Road, Ringmahon, Cork	P: 021-4357679	info@mahon. barnardos.ie sarah.blows@ barnardos.ie	Barnardos
Carmel Devaney Project Leader	**Ballybane**	Ballybane Family Services, Ballybane Com- munity Resource Centre, Ballybane, Galway	P: 091-768123 091-768294 F: 091-773664 087-2072997	ballybanefs@ hotmail.com	Health Board
Eileen O'Toole Project Leader Michelle Moran (acting PL)	**Westside**	Westside Family Services, 189 Corrib Park, Newcastle, Galway	P: 091-585011	westsidefs@ eircom.net eileenotoole@ mailm.hse.ie	Health Board
Paul Tannian Project Leader	**Ballin- foyle**	Ballinfoyle Neighbourhood Youth Project, 60 Ballinfoyle Park, Headford Road, Galway	P: 091-760330 F: 091-760339 M: 087-2072989	ballinfoylenyp @eircom.net	Foróige
Dolores Carroll Project Leader	**Darndale**	Darndale/Belcamp Springboard Project, c/o Our Lady Immaculate Junior School, Darndale, Dublin 17	P: 01-8771712 01-8771713 F : 01-8770772	sboard darndale@ eircom.net dolores.carroll @docharity.net	Daughters of Charity

Tara Kelly Project Leader Sarah Goodwin (Acting P/L)	**Lough- linstown & Bal- lybrack**	Springboard, 8 Laurel Avenue, Ballybrack, Co Dublin	P: 01-2814934 01-2814935 F: 01-2115468 M: 087-9074472	springboardbal lybrack@ hotmail.com	Health Board
Linda Bradley Project Leader	**Raphoe**	Raphoe Spring- board Project, Castle Grove, Raphoe, Co Donegal	P: 074-9173918 074-9173957 F: 074-9173918	springbrdraph @eircom.net	Health Board
Breda Collins Project Leader	**Island- gate Limerick**	Islandgate Family Support Project, 21 Bishop Street, Limerick	P: 061-493588 F: 061-493587 M: 087-2037090	breda.collins@ islandgate. barnardos.ie	Barnardos
Brian Wood Project Leader	**Finglas**	Finglas Family Support Project, 10 Barry Close, Finglas West, Dublin 11	P: 01-8642433 F: 01-8642430 M: 086-1714344	info@ barryclose. barnardos.ie brian.wood@ barnardos.ie	Barnardos
Chris Lawrence Project Leader	**Arklow**	Arklow Spring- board Project, 27 Ferrybank, Arklow, Co Wicklow	P : 0402-24828 F: 0402-31775 M: 087-2771665	springboard1@ eircom.net	Health Board
Ger Phillips	**Spring- board North Lee**	Springboard, 16 Cushing Road, Farrannee, Cork City	P: 021-4305300 F: 021-4305301 M: 087-4109094	phillipsg@ shb.ie	Health Board
Áine Geoghegan	**Fatima Youth Initiative**	Fatima Youth Initiative, 6H Fatima Mansions, Rialto, Dublin 8	P: 01-4539225 F: 01-4539226	fatimayouth initiative@ yahoo.ie	Limited Company

Appendix B

Framework for the Measurement of Social Capital in the UK

Views about the area

(AreaLive) How long have you lived in this area?
1. Less than 12 months
2. 12 months but less than 2 years
3. 2 years but less than 3 years
4. 3 years but less than 5 years
5. 5 years but less than 10 years
6. 10 years but less than 20 years
7. 20 years or longer
8. Don't know

(SatLive) How satisfied are you with this area as a place to live?
SHOW CARD
1. Very satisfied
2. Fairly satisfied
3. Neither satisfied nor dissatisfied
4. Slightly dissatisfied
5. Very dissatisfied
6. (SPONTANEOUS) Don't know

Views about the neighbourhood

(Nintro) Now I'd like to ask you a few questions about your immediate neighbourhood, by which I mean your street or block.

(Neigh Typ) In general, what kind of neighbourhood would you say you live in – would you say it is a neighbourhood in which people do things together and try to help each other, or one in which people mostly go their own way?
1. Help each other
2. Go own way
3. (SPONTANEOUS) Mixture
4. (SPONTANEOUS) Don't know

(Nbackg) To what extent do you agree or disagree that this neighbourhood is a place where people from different backgrounds get on well together?
1. Definitely agree
2. Tend to agree
3. Tend to disagree
4. Definitely disagree
5. DON'T KNOW
6. TOO FEW PEOPLE IN NEIGHBOURHOOD
7. ALL SAME BACKGROUND

(NTrust) Would you say that
1. Most of the people in your neighbourhood can be trusted
2. Some can be trusted
3. A few can be trusted
4. Or that no-one can be trusted
5. (SPONTANEOUS) Just moved here
6. (SPONTANEOUS) Don't know

(SLost) Suppose you lost your (purse/wallet) containing your address details, and it was found in the street by someone living in this neighbourhood. How likely is it that it would be returned to you with nothing missing?
1. Very likely

2. Quite likely
3. Not very likely
4. Or not at all likely
5. Don't know

(PbIntro) I am going to read out a list of problems which some people face in their neighbourhood. For each one, please can you tell me how much of a problem it is.

(Drunk) How much of a problem are people being drunk or rowdy in public places?
SHOW CARD
1. Very big problem
2. Fairly big problem
3. Not a very big problem
4. Not a problem at all
5. It happens but it's not a problem
6. (SPONTANEOUS) Don't know

(Rubbish) How much of a problem is rubbish or litter lying around?

(Vandals) How much of a problem are vandalism, graffiti and other deliberate damage to property or vehicles?

(Drug Use) How much of a problem are people using or dealing drugs?

(Race) How much of a problem is people being attacked or harassed because of their skin colour, ethnic origin or religion?

(Teenhang) How much of a problem are teenagers hanging around on the street?

(AntiNgh) How much of a problem are troublesome neighbours?

Participation in local issues

(InfArea) To what extent do you agree or disagree with the following statements:

I can influence decisions affecting my local area?
SHOW CARD
1. Strongly agree
2. Agree
3. Neither agree nor disagree
4. Disagree
5. Strongly disagree
6. (SPONTANEOUS) Don't have an opinion
7. (SPONTANEOUS) Don't know

(InfNgh) By working together, people in my area can influence decisions that affect the local area?
1. Strongly agree
2. Agree
3. Neither agree nor disagree
4. Disagree
5. Strongly disagree
6. (SPONTANEOUS) Don't have an opinion
7. (SPONTANEOUS) Don't know

(SolvLP) In the last 12 months have you taken any of the following actions in an attempt to solve a problem affecting people in your local area?

SHOW CARD
1. Contacted a local radio station, television station or newspaper
2. Contacted the appropriate organisation to deal with the problem, such as the council
3. Contacted a local councillor or MP
4. Attended a public meeting or neighbourhood forum to discuss local issues
5. Attended a tenants' or local residents' group
6. Attended a protest meeting or joined an action group
7. Helped organise a petition on a local issue
8. No local problems
9. None of the above
10. (SPONTANEOUS) Don't know

Participation in national issues

(SolvNP) In the last 12 months have you taken any of the following actions to show your concern over a national issue?

SHOW CARD
1. Contacted a radio station, television station or newspaper
2. Contacted the appropriate organisation to deal with the problem
3. Contacted an MP
4. Attended a public meeting
5. Attended a protest meeting or joined an action group
6. Helped organise a petition
7. None of these
8. (SPONTANEOUS) Don't know

(Vote) Can I check, did you vote ...
1. ...in the last general election (national election)?
2. (Did you vote) ...in the last local council election?
3. DID NOT VOTE IN EITHER ELECTION
4. NOT ELIGIBLE TO VOTE IN EITHER
5. Don't know

Trust

(Ptrust) Another topic we are interested in is trust. Generally speaking, would you say that most people can be trusted, or that you can't be too careful in dealing with people?
1. Most people can be trusted
2. Can't be too careful in dealing with people
3. It depends on the people/circumstances
4. Don't know

(TrIntro) For the following, please can you tell me how much you trust them
1. Can you tell me how much you trust the police? (Police)
2. Can you tell me how much you trust the courts (Magistrates Courts and Crown Court)? (Courts)
3. Can you tell me how much you trust Parliament? (Parlmnt)

4. (Can you tell me how much you trust the Welsh Assembly? Wales only)
5. (Can you tell me how much you trust the Scottish Executive? Scotland only)
6. Can you tell me how much you trust your local council? (LocC)

SHOW CARD
1. A lot
2. A fair amount
3. Not very much
4. Not at all
5. (SPONTANEOUS) No experience
6. (SPONTANEOUS) Don't know

Social networks

The next few questions are about how often you personally contact your relatives, friends and neighbours. Not counting the people you live with, how often do you do any of the following?
1. Speak to relatives on the phone (Spkrel)
2. Write a letter or note to relatives (Wrtrel)
3. Text or email relatives, or use chatrooms on the internet to talk to relatives (Txtrel)
4. Speak to friends on the phone (Spkfr)
5. Write a letter or note to friends (Wrtfr)
6. Text or email friends, or use chatrooms on the internet to talk to friends (Txtfr)
7. Speak to neighbours (Spkng)

SHOW CARD
1. On most days
2. Once or twice a week
3. Once or twice a month
4. Less often than once a month
5. Never
6. (SPONTANEOUS) Don't know

(FreqMtR) How often do you meet up with relatives who are not living with you?
SHOW CARD

(FreqMtF) How often do you meet up with friends?
SHOW CARD

Social support

(SitIntro) I am going to describe two situations where people might need help. For each one, could you tell me if there is anyone you could ask for help?
(IF MORE THAN ONE PERSON IN HOUSEHOLD ADD: Please include people living with you and people outside the household)
      1. You are ill in bed and need help at home. Is there anyone you could ask for help? Yes/No (Illbed)
      2. You are in financial difficulty and need to borrow money to see you through the next few days. Is there anyone you could ask for help? Yes/No (Money)

If Illbed = Yes then WhoHelp; If Money =Yes then WhoHelp2
(WhoHelp/Whohelp2) Please can you look at this card and tell me who you could ask for help?
SHOW CARD
      1. Husband/wife/partner
      2. Other household member
      3. Relative (outside household)
      4. Friend
      5. Neighbour
      6. Work colleague
      7. Voluntary or other organisation
      8. Other
      9. Would prefer not to ask for help
      10. (SPONTANEOUS) Don't know

(PCrisis) If you had a serious personal crisis, how many people, if any, do you feel you could turn to for comfort and support?
INTERVIEWER: IF MORE THAN 15, CODE AS 15.
(0 – 15, Don't know)

Involvement in groups, clubs and organisations

(GrpIntro) The next questions are about involvement in groups, clubs and organisations. These could be formally organised or just groups of people who get together to do an activity or talk about things. Please exclude just paying a subscription, giving money and anything that was a requirement of your job.

(Intro2) I am going to ask about 3 different types of groups:
First, in the last 12 months, have you been involved with any groups of people who get together to do an activity or to talk about things? These could include evening classes, support groups, slimming clubs, keep-fit classes, pub teams and so on.
(If Intro2 = Yes) then:
(GrpInf) Please can you look at this card. Which of the categories on this card best describe the groups you have taken part in?
SHOW CARD
    1. Hobbies/social clubs
    2. Sports/exercise groups, including taking part, coaching or going to watch
    3. Local community or neighbourhood groups
    4. Groups for children or young people
    5. Adult education groups
    6. Groups for older people
    7. Environmental groups
    8. Health, disability and welfare groups
    9. Political groups
    10. Trade union groups
    11. Religious groups, including going to a place of worship or belonging to a religious based group
    12. Other group
    13. (SPONTANEOUS) None of these
    14. (SPONTANEOUS) Don't know

(Intro3) Second, in the last 12 months, have you taken part in any (other) group activities as part of a local or community group, club or organisation? These could include residents' associations, parent-teacher associations, school or religious groups and so on.

(If Intro3 = yes) then:
(GrpLoc) Please can you look at this card. Which of the categories on this card best describe the groups you have taken part in?

(Intro4) And third, in the last 12 months, have you taken part in any (other) group activities as part of a national group, club or organisation? These could include pressure groups, charities, political groups, environmental groups and so on.
(If Intro4 = yes) then:
(GrpNat) Please can you look at this card. Which of the categories on this card best describe the groups you have taken part in?

Unpaid help to groups and individuals

(DoVolWk) During the last 12 months have you given any unpaid help to any groups, clubs or organisations in any of the ways shown on this card?
SHOW CARD
1. Raising or handling money/taking part in sponsored events
2. Leading the group/member of a committee
3. Organising or helping to run an activity or event
4. Visiting people
5. Befriending or mentoring people
6. Giving advice/information/counselling
7. Secretarial, admin or clerical work
8. Providing transport/driving
9. Representing
10. Campaigning
11. Other practical help (e.g. helping out at school, religious group, shopping)
12. Any other help
13. NONE OF THE ABOVE
14. (SPONTANEOUS) Don't know

(VolFreq) Thinking about the unpaid help you have mentioned, would you say you give this kind of help ...
CODE FIRST THAT APPLIES

1. At least once a week
2. At least once a month
3. At least once every three months
4. Or less often?
5. Other
6. Don't know

(If Less Often or Other at VolFreq) then:
(VolOther) ASK OR RECORD

About how many times in the last 12 months have you given unpaid help through a group, club or organisation?

(Care) Some people have extra responsibilities because they look after someone who has long-term physical or mental ill health or disability, or problems due to old age.
May I check, is there anyone living with you who is sick, disabled or elderly, whom you look after or give special help to, other than in a professional capacity. (For example, a sick or disabled (or elderly) relative/husband/wife/child/friend/parent etc.)

1. Yes
2. No

(HlpGiv) Now I'd like to talk about any unpaid help you may have given people who do not live with you. In the past month have you given any unpaid help in any of the ways shown on the card. Please do not count any help you gave through a group, club or organisation.
SHOW CARD

1. Domestic work, home maintenance or gardening
2. Provision of transport or running errands
3. Help with childcare or babysitting
4. Teaching, coaching or giving practical advice
5. Giving emotional support
6. Other
7. (SPONTANEOUS) Don't know

(HlpInt) Now I'd like to talk about any unpaid help you may have received. In the past month have you received any unpaid help in any of

the ways shown on the card. Please do not count help from people who live with you or from an organisation or group.
SHOW CARD
1. Domestic work, home maintenance or gardening
2. Provision of transport or running errands
3. Help with child care or babysitting
4. Teaching, coaching or giving practical advice
5. Giving emotional support
6. Other
7. (SPONTANEOUS) Don't know

CORE QUESTIONS

Problems in the neighbourhood (views about the area)

(Nintro) Now I'd like to ask you a few questions about your immediate neighbourhood, by which I mean your street or block.

(SLost) Suppose you lost your (purse/wallet) containing your address details, and it was found in the street by someone living in this neighbourhood. How likely is it that it would be returned to you with nothing missing?
1. Very likely
2. Quite likely
3. Not very likely
4. Or not at all likely
5. Don't know

(Drunk) How much of a problem are people being drunk or rowdy in public places?
SHOW CARD
1. Very big problem
2. Fairly big problem
3. Not a very big problem
4. Not a problem at all

5. It happens but it's not a problem
6. (SPONTANEOUS) Don't know

(Rubbish) How much of a problem is rubbish or litter lying around?

(Vandals) How much of a problem are vandalism, graffiti or other deliberate damage to property or vehicles?

(DrugUse) How much of a problem are people using or dealing drugs?

(Race) How much of a problem is people being attacked or harassed because of their skin colour, ethnic origin or religion?

(Teenhang) How much of a problem are teenagers hanging around on the street?

(AntiNgh) How much of a problem are troublesome neighbours?

Participation in local issues (civic participation)

(SolvLP) In the last 12 months have you taken any of the following actions in an attempt to solve a problem affecting people in your local area?
SHOW CARD

1. Contacted a local radio station, television station or newspaper
2. Contacted the appropriate organisation to deal with the problem, such as the council
3. Contacted a local councillor or MP
4. Attended a public meeting or neighbourhood forum to discuss local issues
5. Attended a tenants' or local residents' group
6. Attended a protest meeting or joined an action group
7. Helped organise a petition on a local issue
8. No local problems
9. None of the above
10. (SPONTANEOUS) Don't Know

Contacts with friends, relatives and neighbours (social networks and support)

The next questions are about how often you personally contact relatives, friends and neighbours.
How often do you …
Speak to relatives on the phone (Spkrel)
Speak to friends on the phone (Spkfr)
And how often do you speak to neighbours (face-to-face) (Spkng)
How often do you meet up with relatives who are not living with you? (FreqMtR)
SHOW CARD
1. On most days
2. Once or twice a week
3. Once or twice a month
4. Less often than once a month
5. Never
6. (SPONTANEOUS) Don't know

Unpaid help to groups (social participation)

(DoVolWk) During the last 12 months have you given any unpaid help to any groups, clubs or organisations in any of the ways shown on this card?
SHOW CARD
1. Raising or handling money/taking part in sponsored events
2. Leading the group/member of a committee
3. Organising or helping to run an activity or event
4. Visiting people
5. Befriending or mentoring people
6. Giving advice/information/counselling
7. Secretarial, admin or clerical work
8. Providing transport/driving
9. Representing
10. Campaigning
11. Other practical help (e.g. helping out at school, religious group, shopping)
12. Any other help

13. None of the above
14. (SPONTANEOUS) Don't know

Reciprocity and trust

SLost – this question also measures trust but is positioned earlier in the set because it relates to the neighbourhood.

References

Ahern, B. (2005), 'Task Force to Promote Citizen Participation', *Irish Times*, 15 April.

Aitcheson, A. and Hodgkinson, J. (2003), 'Patterns of Crime in England and Wales' in J. Simmons and T. Dodd (eds.), *Crime in England and Wales 2002–2003*, London: Home Office.

Aldgate, J. and Tunstill, J. (1995), *Making Sense of Section 17: Implementing Services for Children in Need*, London: HMSO.

Area Development Management Ltd. (2005), *Rapid Programme*, Dublin: Department of Community Rural and Gaeltacht Affairs.

Association of Directors of Social Services/National Children Homes (1996), *Children Still in Need – Refocusing Child Protection in the Context of Children in Need*, London: NCH/ADSS.

Attwood, Chris, Gurchand, Singh, Prime, Duncan *et al.* (2003), *2001 Home Office Citizenship Survey: People, Families and Communities* (Home Office Research Study 270), September, London: Home Office, available from: <http://www.homeoffice.gov.uk/rds/pdfs2/hors270.pdf>, accessed 20 June 2007.

Audit Commission (1994), *Seen but Not Heard: Co-ordinating Community Health and Social Services for Children in Need*, London: HMSO.

Barclay, P. (1982), *Social Workers: Their Role and Tasks*, London: Bedford Square Press.

Barnardos (2005), *I'm Still Hungry – Seven Steps to Ending Child Poverty*, Dublin: Barnardos.

Barron, S., Field, J. and Schuller, T. (2000), *Social Capital: Critical Perspectives*, Oxford: Oxford University Press.

Baum, F.E., Bush, R.A., Modra, C.C. *et al.* (2000), 'Epidemiology of Participation: An Australian Community Study', *Journal of Epidemiology and Community Health*, 53(4), 195–6.

Bauman, Z. (2005), *Work, Consumerism and the New Poor*, UK: Open University Press.

Beck, U. (2000), 'Living Your Own Life in a Runaway World: Individualisation, Globalisation and Politics', in W. Hutton and A. Giddens (eds.), *On the Edge: Living with Global Capitalism*, London: Jonathan Cape.

Beck, U. (1992), *The Risk Society*, London: Sage.

Becker, H. (1963), *Outsiders: Studies in the Sociology of Deviance*, Glencoe: Free Press.

Black, A. and Hughes, P. (2001), 'The Identification and Analysis of Indicators of Community Strength and Outcomes' (Occasional Paper No. 3), Department of Family and Community Services, Australia.

Blair, T. (2001), 'Third Way, Phase Two', *Prospect*, 61, 10–13.

Blaxter, L., Hughes, C. and Tight, M. (2001), *How to Research* (2nd rev. edition), UK: Open University Press.

Bourdieu, P. (1986), 'The Forms of Capital' in J.G. Richardson (ed.), *Handbook of Theory and Research for the Sociology of Education*, Greenwood Press: New York.

Bourdieu, P. and Wacquant, L. (1992), *An Invitation to Reflexive Sociology*, Chicago: University of Chicago Press.

Brennan, G. and Pettit, P. (2004), *The Economy of Esteem*, Oxford: Oxford University Press.

Briar-Lawson, K., Lawson, H.A. , Hennon, C.B. and Jones, A.R. (2001), *Family-Centred Policies and Practices: International Implications*, New York: Columbia University Press.

Brooks-Gunn, J., Duncan, G. and Aber, J.L. (1997), *Neighbourhood Poverty: Context and Consequences for Children* (vol. 1); *Policy Implications for Studying Neighbourhoods* (vol. 2), New York: Russell Sage Foundation.

Bronfbrenner, U. (1979), *The Ecology of Human Development*, Boston: Harvard University Press.

Bullen, P. and Onyx, J. (1999), *Social Capital: Family Support Services and Neighbourhood and Community Centres in New South Wales*, Sydney: Family Support Services Association of NSW.

Cannan, C. and Warren, C. (1997), *Social Action with Children and Families*, London: Routledge.

Cass, B. and Cappo, P. (1995), 'Families: Agents and Beneficiaries of Socio-Economic Development', paper presented at the United Nations Inter-regional Meeting of National Coordinators of the International Year of the Family, Bratislava Slovakia, February.

Cattell, V. (2004), 'Social Networks as Mediators Between the Harsh Circumstances of People's Lives, and their Lived Experiences of Health and Well-being', in C. Phillipson, G. Allen and D. Morgan (eds.), *Social Networks and Social Exclusion*, London: Aldgate, 142–162.

Central Statistics Office (2006), Preliminary Reports on the 2006 Census of Population, available at: <http://www.cso.ie/census/Census2006Results.htm>, accessed 20 June 2007.

Central Statistics Office (2004), *Statistical Yearbook of Ireland*, Dublin: The Stationery Office.

Chaskin, R.J. (2006), 'Family Support as Community-based Practice: Considering a Community Capacity Framework for Family Support Provision', in P. Dolan, J. Canavan and J. Pinkerton (eds.) *Family Support as Reflective Practice*, London: Jessica Kingsley Publishers, 42–61.

Children's Bureau (US Department of Health and Human Services) (2000), 'Community Collaborations: A Growing Promise in Child Welfare', *Best Practice/Next Practice*, (1)(2), 1–3.

Children's Bureau (US Department of Health and Human Services) (2000), 'A New Era of Family-Centred Practice', *Best Practice/Next Practice*, (1)(1), 1–6.

Children's Bureau (US Department of Health and Human Services) (2000), *Rethinking Child Welfare Practice under the Adoption and Safe Families Act of 1997*, Washington DC: US Government Printing Office.

Coleman, J.S. (1988), 'Social Capital in the Creation of Human Capital', *American Journal of Sociology*, 94, 95–120.

Coleman, J.S., Campbell, E.Q. , Hobson, C.J. *et al.* (1966), *Equality of Educational Opportunity*, Washington: US Government Printing Office.

Colton, M., Dounz, C. and Williams, M. (1995), *Children in Need*, Aldershot: Avebury.

Commission on the Family (1998), *Strengthening Families for Life*, Dublin: The Stationery Office.

Commission on Social Justice (1994), *Strategies for National Renewal*, London: Vintage.

Cooper, H., Arber, S., Fee, L. and Ginn, J. (1999), *The Influence of Social Support and Social Capital on Health: A Review and Analysis of British Data*, London: Health Education Authority.

Corrigan, C. (2006), *The Development and Implementation of Child Impact Statements in Ireland*, Dublin: Office of the Minister for Children.

Crow, G. (2004), 'Social Networks and Social Exclusion: An Overview of the Debate', in C. Phillipson, G. Allan and D. Morgan, (eds.) *Social Networks and Social Exclusion*, London: Aldgate, 7–20.

Cullen, Elizabeth (2006), 'Growth and the Celtic Cancer: Unprecedented Growth but for Whose Benefit?' in T. O'Connor and M. Murphy (eds.), *Social Care in Ireland: Theory, Policy and Practice* (eds.), Cork: CIT Press, 141–161.

Cummins, J. (2006), 'Measuring Social Capital in Camden', in H. Khan and R. Muir (eds.), *Sticking Together – Social Capital and Local Government*, London: IPPR and Camden, 31–38.

Daly, Mary (2004), *Families and Family Life in Ireland: Challenges for the Future*, Dublin: Department of Social and Family Affairs.

Department for Education and Skills (DfES) (2003), *Every Child Matters* (Green Paper), London: the Stationery Office.

Department for Education and Skills (DfES) (2004), *Every Child Matters: The Next Steps* (Green Paper), London: the Stationery Office.

Department of Health (2001), *Quality and Fairness – A Health System for You*, Dublin: Government Publications.

Department of Health (England) (1995), *Child Protection: Messages from Research*, London: HMSO.

Department of Health (England) (2002), *Health Survey for England 2000: The General Health of Old People and their use of Health Services*, London: The Stationery Office, available at: <http://www.archive2.official-documents.co.uk>, accessed 14 May 2007.

Department of Health (England) (1989), *An Introduction to The Children Act 1989*, London: HMSO.

Dolan, P., Pinkerton, J. and Canavan, J. (2006), 'Family Support: From Description to Reflection', in P. Dolan, J. Canavan and J. Pinkerton (eds.), *Family Support as Reflective Practice*, London: Jessica Kingsley Publishers, 11–23.

Dublin Docklands Development Authority (2003), 'Master Plan', Dublin: DDA, available at: <http://www.ddda.ie/files/publications/20070612022912_Part201[1]. pdf>, accessed 4 June 2007.

Dunst, C. (1995), *Key Characteristics and Features of Community-Based Family Support Programmes*, Chicago: Family Resource Coalition.

Durkheim, E. (1952), *Suicide: A Study in Sociology*, London: Routledge.

Edwards, B. (2005), 'Does it take a Village? An Investigation of Neighbourhood Effects on Australian Children's Development', *Family Matters*, 72, Summer, 36–43.

Edwards, B. (2006), 'Views of the Village: Parents' Perceptions of their Neighbourhoods', *Family Matters*, 74, 26–33.

Expert Group on Mental Health Policy (2006), *A Vision for Change*, Dublin: Stationery Office.

FaCSIA (2004), *Evaluation of the Stronger Families and Communities Strategy 2000–2004: Evaluation Reports*, Department of Families, Community Services and Indigenous Affairs, Australia, available at: <http://www. facsia. gov. au/internet/facsinternet.nsf>, 20 June 2006.

Family Support Agency (2005), *Promoting and Supporting Family and Community Well-being*, Dublin: Family Support Agency.

Family Support Services Association of New South Wales (1999), *Family Support Services in New South Wales*, Sydney: FSSA.

Field, J. (2003), *Social Capital*, London: Routledge.

Finnerty, K. and Collins, B. (2005), 'Social Care and Disability' in P. Share and N. McElwee (eds.), *Applied Social Care*, Dublin: Gill and Macmillan, 271–288.

Fitzgerald, A. (2004), *Shanakill Family Resource Centre 1984–2004: Twenty Years of Growing*, Tralee: Shanakill Family Centre.

Frazer, E. (1999), *The Problems of Communitarian Politics*, Oxford: Oxford University Press.

Frost, N. (1997), 'Delivering Family Support: Issues and Themes in Service Development' in N. Parton (ed.), *Child Protection and Family Support*, London: Routledge, 193–212.

Fukuyama, F. (2001), 'Social Capital, Civil Society and Development', *Third World Quarterly*, 22(1), 7–20.

Fukuyama, F. (1995), *Trust: The Social Virtues and the Creation of Prosperity*, London: Hamish Hamilton.

Furedi, F. (2002), 'For the Greater Good of My CV', *Times Higher Educational Supplement*, 27 September.

Germain, C. (1979), 'Ecology and Social Work', in Germain, C. (ed.), *Social Work Practice: People and Environments*, New York: Columbia University Press, 1–22.

Giddens, A. (1995), *Sociology*, Cambridge: Polity Press.

Giddens, A. (1998), *The Third Way*, Cambridge: Polity Press.

Gilchrist, A. (2004), *The Well-Connected Community: A Networking Approach to Community Development*, Bristol: The Policy Press.

Gilligan, R. (1995), 'Family Support and Child Welfare: Realising the Promise of the Child Care Act 1991', in H. Ferguson and K. Kenny (eds.), *On Behalf of the Child, Child Welfare, Child Protection and the Child Care Act 1991*, Dublin: Farmar & Farmar, 60–84.

Gilligan, R. (1991), *Irish Child Care Services*, Dublin: IPA.

Gilligan, R. (2000), 'Working with Social Networks – Key Resources in Helping Children at Risk', in M. Hill (ed.), *Effective Ways of Working with Children and Families*, London: Jessica Kingsley Publishers.

Glass, N. (1999), 'Sure Start: the Development of an Early Intervention Programme for Young Children in the United Kingdom', *Children and Society*, 13(4), 257–264.

Goldson, B. (2001), 'The Demonization of Children: from the Symbolic to the Institutional', in P. Foley, J. Roche and S. Tucker (eds.), *Children in Society – Contemporary Theory, Policy and Practice*, Basingstoke: Palgrave Macmillan, 34–42.

Granovetter, M. (1974), *Getting a Job: A Study of Contacts and Careers*, Cambridge MA: Harvard University Press.

Hagan, J. and McCarthy, B. (1997), *Mean Streets: Youth Crime and Homelessness*, Cambridge: Cambridge University Press.

Hall, P.A. (1999), 'Social Capital in Britain', *British Journal of Political Science*, 29(3), 417–61.

Halpern, D. (2005), *Social Capital*, Cambridge: Polity Press.

Hardiker, P., Exton, K. and Barker, M. (1991), 'The Social Policy Context of Prevention in Child Care', *British Journal of Social Work*, 21, 341–359.

Harper, R. and Kelly, M. (2003), *Measuring Social Capital in the United Kingdom*, London: United Kingdom Office for National Statistics.

Hearn, B. (1997), 'Putting Child and Family Support into Practice', in Parton, N. (ed.) *Child Protection and Family Support*, London: Routledge, 223–242.

Henderson, P. and Thomas, D.N. (2002), *Skills in Neighbourhood Work*, London: Routledge.

Hendryx, M.S., Ahern, M.M., Lovrich, N.P. and McCurdy, A.H. (2002), 'Access to Health Care and Community Social Capital', *Health Services Research*, 37(1), 87–103.

Hirschman, A.O. (1984), *Getting Ahead Collectively: Grassroots Experiences in Latin America*, New York: Pergamon Press.

HM Treasury (1998), *Comprehensive Spending Review: Cross Departmental Review of Provision for Children*, London: HM Treasury.

Hodge, P. (1970), 'The Future of Community Development' in W. Robson and B. Crick (eds.), *The Future of the Social Services*, Middlesex: Penguin, 66–81.

Holman, R. (1978), *Poverty*, Oxford: Martin Robinson.

Houston, A.E. (2005), 'The Impact of Sure Start – The Returns', paper given at the 'Whither Social Capital? Past, Present and Future' Conference, South Bank University, April 6–7.

Humphreys, E. (2005), 'Social Capital: Mediating Conditions to Create "Successful" Neighbourhoods?', paper given at Symposium on Civic and Social Life in the Suburbs, NUI Maynooth, 8 April 2005.

Irish Examiner (2004), 'Locking Children Up is not the Key to Cutting Crime', 19 May.

Irish Times (2005), 'Ban "Hoodies" from Shopping Centres', 10 November.

Irish Times (2005), 'A Long, Long Way from the Nest', 29 October.

Irish Times (2006), 'High Court Rules against Lesbian Couple', 15 December.

Jack, G. (2000), 'Ecological Influences on Parenting and Child Development', *British Journal of Social Work*, 30(6), 703–720.

Jack, G. (2001), 'An Ecological Perspective on Child Abuse', in F. Foley, J. Roche and S. Tucker (eds.), *Children and Society*, UK: Open University Press, 185–195.

Jack, G. and Gill, O. (2003), *The Missing Side of the Triangle*, Essex: Barnardos.

Jack, G. and Jordan, B. (1999), 'Social Capital and Child Welfare', *Children and Society*, 13(4), 242–256.

Jackson, C.M. and Heffernan, C.M. (2004), 'A Qualitative Study of Public Perspectives on Family Support Services in Ireland', *Irish Journal of Applied Social Studies*, 5(1&2), Summer and Winter, 33–50.

Jordan, B. (1997), 'Partnership with Service Users in Child Protection and Family Support', in N. Parton (ed.), *Child Protection and Family Support*, London: Routledge, 212–223.

Jordan, B. (2007), *Social Work and Well-Being*, Lyme Regis: Russell House Publishing.

Kawachi, I., Kennedy, B.P., Lochner, K. and Prothrow-Stith, D. (1997), 'Social Capital, Income Inequality and Mortality', *American Journal of Public Health*, 89(9), 1491–1498.

Keaney, E. (2006), *From Access to Participation – Cultural Policy and Civil Renewal*, London: Institute for Public Policy Research.

Keenan, O. (1996), *Kelly: A Child is Dead*, Dublin: Stationery Office.

Kelleher, C. and Kelleher, P. (1997), *Family Resource Centres*, Dublin: The Stationery Office.

Kohen, D.E, Brooks-Gunn, J.B. , Leventhal, T. and Hertzman C. (2002), 'Neighborhood Income and Physical and Social Disorder in Canada: Associations with Young Children Competencies', *Child Development*, 73, 1844–60.

Laming, Lord (2003), *The Victoria Climbie Inquiry Report* (CM 5730), London: The Stationery Office.

Lee, N. (2001), *Childhood and Society: Growing up in an Age of Uncertainty*, UK: Open University Press.

Madonna House Inquiry Committee (1996), *Report into Child Abuse in Madonna House*, Dublin: The Stationery Office.

Marsh, I. and Keating, M. (2000), *Sociology: Making Sense of Society*, Harlow: Prentice Hall.

McGahern, J. (2005), *Memoir*, London: Faber and Faber.

McGrath, B. (2003), *Assessing the Community Development-Family Support Relationship: An Exploratory Examination of Projects and Programmes in the West of Ireland*, Western Health Board/NUI Galway.

McGuinness, C. (1993), *The Report of the Kilkenny Incest Investigation*, Dublin: The Stationery Office.

McKeown, K. (1999), 'Evaluation: A Guide to its Language and Logic', *Administration*, 47(1), Spring , 30–41.

References

McKeown, K. (2001), *Springboard: Promoting Family Well-being through Family Support Services*, Dublin: Department of Health and Children.

Merton, R.K., (1957), *Social Theory and Social Structure*, Glencoe: Free Press.

Miller, L.B. and Bentovim, A. (2003), 'Assessing Families: the Family Assessment of Family Competence, Strengths and Difficulties', in M. Bell, and K. Wilson, (eds.), *The Practitioner's Guide to Working with Families*, Basingstoke: Palgrave, 57–85.

Miller, M., Canavan, J. and Walsh, D. (2002), 'From Value for Money to Practice Improvement and Beyond: Introducing Evaluation to a Voluntary Sector Youth Project', *Administration*, 50(2), Summer, 20–34.

Mills, C.W. (1969), *The Sociological Imagination*, Oxford: Oxford University Press.

Molyneaux, M. (2002), 'Gender and the Silences of Social Capital: Lessons from Latin America', *Development and Change*, 33(2), 167–188.

Mowbray, M. (2005), 'Community Capacity Building or State Opportunism?', *Community Development Journal*, 40(3), July, 255–65.

Muir, R. (2006), 'Social Capital in Camden', in H. Khan and R. Muir (eds.), *Sticking Together: Social Capital and Local Government*, London: IPPR and Camden, 4–25.

Murphy, M. (1996), 'From Prevention to Family Support and Beyond: Promoting the Welfare of Irish Children', *Administration*, 44(2), Summer, 73–101.

National Economic and Social Council (NESC) (1987), *Community Care Services*, report no. 83a, November: Irish Government Publications.

National Economic and Social Council (NESC) (2005), *The Developmental Welfare State*, report no. 113, May, Dublin: Irish Government Publications.

National Economic and Social Forum (NESF) (2003), *The Policy Implications of Social Capital*, forum report no. 28, June, Dublin: Irish Government Publications.

O'Brien, J. and O'Brien, L. (1989), *Framework for Accomplishment*, Georgia: Responsive Systems Associates.

Observer, The (2004), 'Civil Rights Group Challenges Night Curfews for Teenagers', 20 June.

Observer, The (2005), 'Fashion Item or Symbol of Fear', 15 May.

O'Doherty, C. (2003), 'The Future of Social Care Providing Services and Creating Social Capital', *Irish Journal of Applied Social Studies*, 4(2), 33–38.

O'Doherty, C. (2003), 'Shanakill Family Resource Centre: Evaluation', unpublished paper.

O'Doherty, C. (2006), 'Social Care and Social Capital', in T. O'Connor and M. Murphy (eds.), *Social Care in Ireland: Theory, Policy and Practice*, Cork: CIT Press, 25–42.

O'Doherty, C. (2004), *Towards the Construction of an International Model for the Promotion of Child and Family Welfare Practice: Family Support Activities of the Irish Health Boards under the Child Care Act 1991*, unpublished Ph.D. thesis, University College Dublin.

O'Doherty, C. and Farrelly, T., (2006) *Planning and Sustainable Development*, unpublished research study completed for Kerry County Council.

Office for National Statistics (2002), General Household Survey 2001–2002 (Study no. 4646), available at: <http://www.data-archive. ac.uk>, accessed 14 June 2007.

Organisation for Economic Co-operation and Development (2001), *The Well-being of Nations: The Role of Human and Social Capital*, Paris: OECD Publications.

O'Sullivan, E. (2001), 'Children Act 2001', Southern Health Board Seminar, Cork City, 28 September.

Parton, N. (2006), *Safeguarding Childhood*, Basingstoke: Palgrave.

Pithouse, A., Lindsell, S. and Cheung, M. (1998), *Family Support and Family Centre Services*, London: Ashgate.

Putnam, R.D. (2000), *Bowling Alone: The Collapse and Revival of American Community*, New York: Simon and Schuster.

Putnam, R.D. (1993), *Making Democracy Work: Civic Traditions in Modern Italy*, Princeton NJ: Princeton University Press.

Quinton, D. (2004), *Supporting Parents: Messages from Research*, London: Department for Education and Skills and Department of Health.

RMIT University (2004), *Evaluation of the Stronger Families and Community Strategy 2000–2004: Community Capacity Building,*

Melbourne: Department of Family and Community Services/ Australian Government.

RMIT University (2004), *Evaluation of the Stronger Families and Communities Strategy 2000–2004: Gilles Plain Community Garden–A Case Study*, Melbourne: Department of Family and Community Affairs/Australian Government.

RMIT University (2004), *Evaluation of the Stronger Families and Communities Strategy 2000–2004: Networks and Partnerships*, Melbourne: Department of Family and Community Services/ Australian Government.

Sampson, R.J. and Laub, J.H. (1993), *Crime in the Making: Pathways and Turning Points through Life*, Cambridge, MA: Harvard University Press.

Sampson, R.J., Morenoff, J.D and Gannon-Rowley, T. (2002), 'Assessing "Neighbourhood Effects": Social Processes and New Directions in Research', *American Journal of Sociology*, 105(3), 603–651.

Savage, M. (2005), 'Voluntary Associations and Social Capital: Challenging Tocquvillian Perspectives', paper given at 'Whither Social Capital? Past, Present and Future' conference in London South Bank University, 6–7 April .

Schoor, L.B. (1997), *Common Purpose: Strengthening Families and Neighbourhoods to Rebuild America*, New York: Doubleday.

Scott, D. (2001), 'Building Communities that Strengthen Families', *Family Matters*, 58, Autumn, 76–79.

Seebohm Report (1968), Report of the Committee on Local Authority and Allied Personal Social Services, Cmnd. 3703, London: HMSO.

Stone, W. (2001), *Measuring Social Capital*, Melbourne: Australian Institute of Family Studies.

Task Force on Active Citizenship (2007), Report, Dublin: Government Publications.

Task Force on Active Citizenship (2006), *Together, We're Better* (public consultation paper), Dublin: Government Publications.

Task Force on Child Care Services (1980), Final Report, Dublin: the Stationery Office.

Taylor, M. (2004), 'Community Issues and Social Networks', in C. Phillipson, G. Allan and D. Morgan (eds.), *Social Networks and Social Exclusion*, London: Aldgate.

Tovey, H. and Share, P. (2003), *A Sociology of Ireland*, Dublin: Gill and Macmillan.

Tunstill, J., Aldgate, J. and Hughes, M. (2007), *Improving Children's Services Networks*, London: Jessica Kingsley Publishers.

Twelvetrees, A. (1991), *Community Work*, Basingstoke: Macmillan.

United Nations (1989), Convention on the Rights of the Child, 20 November, available at: <http://www.ohchr.org/english/law/pdf/crc.pdf>, accessed 3 July 2007.

United Nations (2005), Ireland's Second Report to the UN Committee on the Rights of the Child, available at: <http://www.childrensrights.ie/pubs/IRLCONCOBS.pdf>, accessed 1 July 2007.

United Nations (1998), 'Observations on the Initial Report on Irish Child Care Services', UN Geneva, 23 January, available at: <http://www.umn.edu/humanrts/crc/ireland1998.html>, accessed 3 July 2007.

Veenstra, G. (2000), 'Social Capital, SES and Health: An Individual Level Analysis', *Social Science and Medicine*, 50(5), 619–629.

Vinson, T., Baldry, E. and Hargreaves, J. (1996), 'Neighbourhoods, Networks and Child Abuse', *The British Journal of Social Work*, 26(4), 523–543.

Warr, D.J. (2005), 'Social Networks in a 'Discredited' Neighbourhood', paper given at 'Whither Social Capital? Past, Present and Future' conference, South Bank University, London, 6–7 April.

Whitehead, M and Diderichsen, F. (2001), 'Social Capital and Health: Tiptoeing through the Minefield of Evidence', *The Lancet*, 358(9277), 165–6.

Wilkinson, R.G. (1996), *Unhealthy Societies: The Afflictions of Inequality*, UK: Routledge.

Wolcott, I. (1989), *Family Support Services: A Review of the Literature and Selected Annotated Bibliography*, Melbourne: Australian Institute of Family Studies.

Woolcock, M. (1998), 'Social Capital and Economic Development: Towards a Theoretical Synthesis and Policy Framework', *Theory and Society*, (27)2, 151–208.

Index

active citizenship 135–144, 150, 151–153
    civic renewal and 137, 142
    European Union (EU) and 140–141
    government and 140–142
    inequality and 138
    Organisation for Economic Co-operation and Development (OECD) and 140–141
    participation in decision making 140–2
    social capital and 137
    volunteering and 138–140
    See also Task Force on Active Citizenship

adolescence 20–1

adult education 32, 53, 55, 60, 67, 100, 101

anti-social behaviour 22, 23–4, 25, 42, 145, 146

Anti-Social Behaviour Act 2003 22, 42, 43
    anti-social behaviour orders (ASBOs) 25, 44

associational life 11, 13

Barnardos 42, 114

Beck, Ulrich 36, 38

best interests of the child 40–44

Bourdieu, Pierre 8–10, 14, 29

Camden local authority 144–7
    Family in Focus schemes 146
    measuring social capital 144, 146

Catholic Church 108

change mapping 123

Children Act 1908 42